Praise for *My Journeys in Economic Theory*

"This gem of a book is the moving and candid memoir by one of the deepest and widest-ranging economists of our time. It is also unusual in laying bare the fits and starts that are an inevitable part of the creative process."

—PARTHA DASGUPTA, AUTHOR OF *TIME AND THE GENERATIONS: POPULATION ETHICS FOR A DIMINISHING PLANET*

"In Edmund Phelps's latest journey, he discovers a revolutionary theory of the good life: Beyond providing leisure and material comforts, a modern economy engages participants in adventure and self-discovery. These profound ideas mesh with his own story, told here beautifully and honestly."

—RICHARD ROBB, AUTHOR OF *WILLFUL: HOW WE CHOOSE WHAT WE DO*

"In this engaging memoir, Phelps takes us on a journey from a childhood and lifelong fascination with creativity to a Nobel Prize and beyond, explaining the why of dynamism, the what of innovation, and the how of rewarding work. A must-read for any lover of economic ideas."

—GLENN HUBBARD, AUTHOR OF *THE WALL AND THE BRIDGE: FEAR AND OPPORTUNITY IN DISRUPTION'S WAKE*

"Phelps has always been one of the most brilliant and most deep-thinking of the economists who came of age in the 1960s. This memoir impresses the reader with how deeply and broadly he has been thinking throughout his career. *My Journeys in Economic Theory* will repair the ignorance of the underappreciated depth of Phelps's contributions."

—J. BRADFORD DELONG, AUTHOR OF *SLOUCHING TOWARDS UTOPIA: AN ECONOMIC HISTORY OF THE TWENTIETH CENTURY*

MY JOURNEYS
IN ECONOMIC
THEORY

MY JOURNEYS IN ECONOMIC THEORY

EDMUND PHELPS

Columbia University Press *New York*

Columbia University Press
Publishers Since 1893
New York   Chichester, West Sussex
cup.columbia.edu

ISBN 9780231207300 (hardback)
ISBN 9780231556910 (ebook)

LCCN: 2022041689

Columbia University Press books are printed on permanent
and durable acid-free paper.
Printed in the United States of America

Cover design: Noah Arlow

To Viviana

CONTENTS

PREFACE

This book tells the story of my role in reshaping aspects of economic theory over the past sixty years—first by putting the employment theory introduced by John Maynard Keynes and John Hicks onto microeconomic foundations and, in the past two decades, by replacing the growth theory of Joseph Schumpeter and Robert Solow with a theory in which innovation and job satisfaction, too, are fueled primarily by the dynamism of a range of people working in the economy.

Yet, these memoirs also tell the story of my personal experiences in my career as an economic theorist: the fierce opponents, the competing claimants, the teacher who underestimated me, the great figures I was fortunate to be close to, and the satisfaction of conceiving a radical departure from the prevailing understanding of innovation, hence economic growth, and, more important, a huge departure from the prevailing perspective on work and life itself.

At the core of my intellectual development has been the excitement of hitting upon a new idea, of exercising my creativity rather than testing or applying others' models. I became a theorist—working at first in the thick of the theorizing that had gained attention in previous decades. At some point, though,

I became aware that all my past theoretical work had been built on breakthroughs of a few other theorists. I had been conceiving new elements with which to support or enrich the basic theories of others rather than conceiving a basic theory of my own. Fortunately, a new perspective on the economy of a modern society developed in my mind, and I was able over the next decade to build a theory of my own.

My early work began with concepts and findings I hit upon in my first half-dozen years or so at Yale's Cowles Foundation for Research in Economics and in my time at the RAND Corporation and Massachusetts Institute of Technology: the Golden Rule (of saving), the harm from public debt, and the effects when investing in capital is "risky." This work ended with the advances made in my half-dozen years at the Wharton School of the University of Pennsylvania and some time at the London School of Economics and in Cambridge: the breakthrough in Keynes's efforts to understand wage behavior (called the "microfoundations of macro") and the concept of an equilibrium unemployment level (or "natural rate" in Milton Friedman's words). All this was well within the realm of standard economics—classical, neoclassical, and Keynesian.

In the next decade, first at Stanford University's Center for Advanced Studies in the Behavioral Sciences (CASBS), then in New York, and soon after at Columbia University, my final home, I began to move away from the central focus of existing economic theory. At CASBS, responding to the discontent demonstrated by women and Black people in the 1960s, I wrote about what I dubbed "statistical discrimination." In New York, I had opportunities to interact with philosophers and intellectuals in the university and in the city on issues of mutual interest. I organized a multidisciplinary conference of leading figures on the practice of altruism and defended it against attacks at the

Chicago Law School. My world expanded as I thought more about social and moral subjects.

John Rawls, who I worked next door to at CASBS, had the greatest influence on my work in those years. His conception of economic justice drew me to produce a paper investigating the tax structure needed to raise the revenue required for Rawlsian economic justice. Following Rawls's book and my paper, society's neglect of the least advantaged workers was always in the back of my mind—and sometimes at the top of my mind. The notion of economic justice in addition to notions of racial and gender equality were new forces in social thought and policy discussion.

In the book that I started at CASBS, I added the argument for drawing people, particularly the less advantaged, into "rewarding work" so that they could experience the dignity and the satisfactions that come from their participation in society's central project: the economy. (Of course, this is a very Western view and explicit in Rawls's great book.) Some three decades later, a growing sense of the experience of work and its profound importance—its centrality to the lives we lead—would have a deep impact on my work.

Other debates and developments came up in the 1980s and more in the 1990s. I couldn't resist challenging the new claim that a stimulus to aggregate demand in a country spills over to trading partners—the "rising tide" view. I was drawn to the recurrent controversy over whether booms and slumps are mainly driven by "structural" forces or by vicissitudes of "aggregate demand"—Keynes versus Friedrich Hayek. With the dissolution of the Soviet Union, I was invited to the ensuing discussion over capitalism and socialism, and, with the stagnation in Italy, I was later enlisted to analyze the weakness of "enterprise and inclusion" in Italy's economy.

Yet the range of contributions for which I was mainly remembered in those years—such as the argument that expectations in real-life economies may be off the mark and the argument that wages in the lowest echelons of the labor force can be pulled up through employment subsidies—began to be remote from the new interests I developed in the new century.

I started to explore a new course: to attempt a rethinking of the theory of innovation that had been introduced by Schumpeter a century earlier in his 1911–1912 book and later taught to Harvard students, such as Solow, who in 1956 incorporated that theory into his "growth model"—a new model that I and every trained economist had to study.

A fresh perspective on the economy—the kind of modern economy that Paul Johnson saw as beginning around 1815 in Britain and first flowered around the late 1850s in the United States and Europe—began to take shape in my mind. When I looked back at the standard theories of my contemporaries (and my theories, too), I began to think it was odd that while I and other economic theorists had been using the creativity that people commonly have, thus the imagination to create new theories and new things, in not one of the existing theoretical models were any of the actors described as exhibiting the slightest creativity! In this respect, my previous theoretical work, like that of all the others' work, had adhered to the premise of existing economics that the actors in the economy possess and exhibit no creativity or have no thought of using whatever creativity they might have. (This economics recognized only the disutility of work, failing to recognize what household surveys term job satisfaction.)

In parallel to that desire to create a theoretical model that was fundamentally mine rather than an extension or improvement of the basic model of another theorist, I became open to recognizing in my own thinking the creativity of people in general. I came to doubt that Schumpeter's theory of innovation came even close to explaining the explosion of productivity growth from the mid-nineteenth to the mid-twentieth century. I felt ready to build a theory based on the desire of a great many people to use their creativity—their ingenuity and imagination.

Early in the first decade of the present century, a new idea on the extraordinary economic success of several Western nations began evolving in my mind. I came to sense that in the societies embracing modern values—such as the societies emerging over the nineteenth century in Britain, then the United States, and soon after Germany and France (to name the large ones)— much and perhaps most of the society's economy was engaged *not* simply in producing existing products and services, drawing on capital and labor inputs and whatever technological advances that scientific discoveries had made possible. People working in companies were also conceiving better ways to produce things and even new things to produce. Thus, massive numbers of people, most of them "ordinary people" (as I like to say) were generating what was in the aggregate an impressive flow of *indigenous* innovation within the nation's economy—that is, innovation coming from inside the nation's businesses (in contrast to *exogenous* innovation—innovation coming from outside the nation or outside the business sector, at any rate). Economists from Schumpeter right up to the present day, still under the influence of neoclassical thinking, could not have imagined that a substantial number of people may possess insights and intuitions (personal knowledge) that could propel an economy forward.

The most obvious reward of such activity in these societies may have been the *material* gains: In these Western nations, Walt Rostow's "take-off into sustained growth" arrived—one after the other. Wages grew, sooner or later, and rates of return on investments in farms and factories rose to new heights. The resulting rise of incomes pulled living standards among the working class and the middle class to unprecedented heights. (If that growth was just the fruit of Schumpeterian innovation, it would not have been so concentrated in just four or five countries.)

What was ultimately more striking was the deep involvement of many businesspeople exercising their imagination to create new methods or new products—a widespread demonstration of creativity. Among these people, there was an extraordinary sense of *flourishing*—meeting challenges and achieving self-expression and personal growth. These *nonmaterial* rewards became for many people no less important than the material rewards of work. Most people need to work to live, but most people also need to express their creativity and talent. In this kind of economy then—hence, the kind of society that nourishes such an economy—ordinary people in exercising their creativity could carve out a kind of life that is far more meaningful than a career devoid of this dimension.

I have come to maintain, then, that an adequate understanding of the directions and achievements in such a country's economy requires delving into the character of the people—in particular, a set of values that foster a willingness and even a desire to explore the unknown and try out the new. The gradual understanding of the phenomenon that I called indigenous innovation—innovation fueled by the creativity of people (and a set of values encouraging its exercise)—breaks new ground in economic theory.

An adequate understanding of people's well-being, however, must recognize also the notion of the good life, which consists of far more than wages, wealth, the amenities of town and country, and the rapid economic growth of these things. It is the business of innovating and the involvement of many employees in discussing, conceiving, and testing a new method or product. A method or product hitherto untested was something new under the sun, yet whole nations were soon engaged in this unprecedented activity. Those countries were soon displaying what I dubbed "mass flourishing."

Readers looking in this book for some sign of personal development in the past two decades can find it in the last chapter. I had left existing models—models in which I provided microfoundations for Keynes's appeal to the "stickiness" of wages, explored the tax structure for Rawls's economic justice, and noticed a problem in Frank Ramsey's theory of optimum saving—for a land not modeled before in which innovating is widespread, job satisfaction is abundant, and the good life is about much more than wealth.

Nothing in my work has given me such pleasure. In conceiving this theory of mass flourishing, I had the enormous satisfaction of making considerable use of my own creativity. In coming to understand the rather widespread phenomenon of meaningful lives, my own life became more meaningful.

This book, then, is not an autobiography—though it has many stories to tell. It is a series of memoirs related to my intellectual and professional journeys over the past sixty years—journeys from my early improvements of existing employment theory, to the creation of a radically new theory of innovation, and on to an understanding of how the process of that innovation (for about a century in the fortunate nations) was for many people the major avenue to meaningful work and the good life.

INTRODUCTION

Formative Years

I was born in July 1933. My mother, father, and I lived in northern Chicago, a few blocks from Lake Michigan on Glenwood Avenue. I was to be an only child, like many kids in those times.

My mother, Florence Esther Stone, the last of eight children, had grown up on a large farm downstate in rural Decatur, Illinois, and had become a nutritionist in Chicago, where she met my father, Edmund Strother Phelps. The son of a prosperous shoe manufacturer and merchant, he had grown up in upstate Illinois and had secured an advertising position in a Chicago bank.

I always thought that my parents were a striking couple. My father was 6′2″ and something of an athlete. Too young to join the U.S. Army to fight in World War I, he had joined the Canadian Army and cut a dashing figure in several photos. My mother, also tall at 5′9″, was not athletic but sturdy. Both of them liked to read and dress well. They used to go out occasionally on Saturday evenings for dinner and dancing at the Edgewater Beach Hotel. My mother was very social, later becoming president of the Parent Teacher Association and then head of the League of Women Voters. When I left each morning for school, she was already on the phone with one of her members. My father liked being in the office with others and making visits to people at other companies.

Both my parents had a college education. My mother studied home economics at James Millikin College (now University) in Decatur, and my father studied some economics and played on the baseball team at the University of Illinois at Champaign-Urbana. Certainly, this background had an influence on my future direction.

An interviewer from Swedish television once assumed that what led me to study economics was my experience of the Great Depression. It is true that both my parents lost their jobs, but I was too young in those years to sense the loss my parents must have felt or to see any hardship they may have suffered. My grandfather, doing well enough in the shoe business, may have helped us out; and my mother's brothers and sisters could also have helped. But, looking back, I can see that my mother and father might have been a lot more joyful had they not lost their jobs.

Yet we were not an unhappy family. I loved running around the apartment and got a lasting scar on my forehead from a bad fall. In the summer, we sometimes went to the beach. An old photo shows me at the shore of Lake Michigan with my bucket and shovel, building castles out of the sand. These were my early impulses: to run around the apartment and to make something.

Perhaps the happiest memory I have of this time is a long walk I took with my father, looking at a few cars on the way, to see the Chicago and North Western Railway train called "The 400" speeding its way from Minneapolis to the Chicago terminal. I could sense the power of the engine. Perhaps my father, although he may not have had the words to describe the world's possibilities, thought this awesome sight would be inspiring to me, which it certainly was.

In the summer of 1939, after placing advertisements in the papers, my father got a job in advertising and sales in New York City. Presumably, he also placed ads in the Chicago papers, but nothing panned out. So, we became easterners. I was excited that Mr. Quigley, the owner of the company, let us have for a few weeks an apartment of his with a marvelous balcony overlooking a spacious living room and, outside, the Hudson River. It gave me a sense of something that would be awfully nice to have.

I sensed that my parents were relieved to have the income that began coming in and my father felt good about having a job. Throughout his life, he showed a love of work—sometimes talking about things coming up at the office.

After some research by my parents about the commuter town with the best school system, we settled in Hastings-on-Hudson, living in a garden apartment complex, Hastings House, on the river's edge looking across to the Palisades. For a six-year-old, the place was fertile ground for my imagination to stretch its legs. (During the war years, the rock formation across from Yonkers some miles downstream resembled Adolf Hitler. A rockslide in 1947 finally wiped it away.) Hasting House was where I lived throughout my early school years. Being so young, my memories of World War II are not very clear—instead, what stands out most to me are those school years from first to twelfth grade.

The Hastings Public School was a godsend. My class had about fifty boys and fifty girls, not too few or too many. I was particularly entranced by Mrs. Murphy, my second-grade teacher, whom I later thanked when I received the Distinguished Fellow medal at the annual meeting of the American Economic Association in 2000 for "teaching me how to read and write."

My class had several interesting students: Paul Perreten later served Hastings as a lawyer, Julie Scott became a successful architect in California who designed the Packard Foundation Building in Los Altos (among other university and office buildings), Lee Snyder became a theologian, Don Maricle became an important chemist who developed the first lithium sulfur-dioxide battery, Sheila Reardon and Bob Brown ended up working in New York, and Judy Sweetland (whose mother sang in movies) went on to work in Hollywood. Although we did not have a strong sense of competition among each other, I knew I had to work some to match them or stay ahead. After school, it so happened that in the northwest corner of Hastings where I lived there was no one my age or close enough in age to play with. I had to find ways to occupy myself.

At age eleven or so, I conducted a poll of the number of cats living in Hastings House—a study long remembered by residents. Later, I was immersed in observing every night on the busy Route 9 running nearby the state on the license plate of each car going by. I was intrigued by the number coming from each state and by the variability of the observed distribution. My parents seemed to take this curiosity in stride, encouraging it where they could.

When I turned fourteen—in the summer of 1947—I met Jim Byrne, who lived across the fence in Dobbs Ferry and was a couple of years older. Together, we conjured up an entire league of baseball teams and played games between his teams and my teams—meticulously recording all the games and the league standings. Initially, these games were played on paper. This was a kind of magic. Later, we played two-man baseball games, pitching to each other. Around this time, I went with my father to my first baseball game, and later we went to see Mel Ott vie against Stan Musial at the Polo Grounds. Another time, I went alone to see Ted Williams hit, facing the newly introduced Boudreau Shift, at Yankee Stadium. I was in awe of those giants.

Being so close to the city, Hastings gave my family access to New York City and the world. Even in the war years, my father commuted to the city every weekday of his long life—he never really retired. We would often go to experience all of the opportunities that a great city affords. We all went to see Irving Berlin's *This Is the Army* with Berlin himself and, later, to see *Oklahoma!* My mother and I sometimes went to Radio City Music Hall to see a movie or the Rockettes. *How Green Was My Valley*, *Phantom of the Opera*, and *Notorious*, among others, made a lasting impression. I was amazed by the style of Cary Grant, marveled at the mystery of Ingrid Bergman, and was shaken by the power of the art form when the mask was ripped off the face of the Phantom, played by Claude Rains. These early excursions to experience the arts laid the foundation for my lifelong appreciation for music and the creativity of the arts, which continues to inspire me today.

Movies were important to me, but so were newspapers, radio, and books. For years, I remembered hearing in 1940 the sepulchral voice of Edward R. Murrow over the radio announcing "this is London" before reporting the latest news on the London Blitz. When my father brought home the daily papers he had read on the train, I looked for reports of the epic battle in the North African theater between General Rommel (the Desert Fox) and Field Marshal Montgomery (Monty). These stories fascinated me and got me started reading the daily papers.

I also started to read books in earnest, having been inspired by my father reading to me *Winnie the Pooh* and *Now We Are Six* when I was little. I began with the books in my father's bookcase: Robert Louis Stevenson's *Treasure Island*, Jack London's *Call of the Wild* and *White Fang*, among many others. They led me to other works such as H. Rider Haggard's *King Solomon's Mines* and *She*, Arthur Conan Doyle's *Adventures of Sherlock Holmes*, and Jules Verne's *Twenty Thousand Leagues Under the Sea*. In my teenage years, I was mesmerized by Thomas Mann's *Magic Mountain*, James Hilton's *Lost Horizon*, Charlotte Brontë's *Jane Eyre*, and Emily Brontë's *Wuthering Heights* as well as a clutch of novels mostly by American authors of that time—Upton Sinclair, Sherwood Anderson, Ernest Hemmingway, John Steinbeck, and Thomas Wolfe. I wanted to have a better idea of what the world is like.

These books—all works of high imagination—surely had a huge impact on me. In fact, my first published paper, "The Golden Rule of Accumulation," was written as a "fable" of a fictitious kingdom in which the inhabitants ("Solovians," named after Robert Solow) have a policy question to answer. I always understood that one can gain insights from analyzing invented people in an invented economy. To attempt to understand the real world, I sensed we have to understand some unreal ones— some abstract representations.

Over these formative years on my way toward high school, I remained close to my parents. I felt their love and was aware of their giving me every advantage they could. My mother was of Puritan stock—her family figured in Sarah Vowell's entertaining history of the Massachusetts Bay Colony, *The Wordy Shipmates*— so work was at the core of her being, and I was her main work until I was through high school. Each day I came home from school, my mother was there with Toll House chocolate chip cookies still warm from the oven. (She took a job—teaching home economics and nutrition in Yonkers—only after I went away to college.) She didn't complain that, after the cookies and a brief exchange, I went straight to dialing radio station WBAI to catch the 1940s jazz led by Charlie Parker, next to looking at any new magazine that had arrived, and then to practicing the trumpet. My mother was unfailingly supportive of me and my father. I often joined her when she went in the car to the train station to meet my father coming back from work.

My father was a shy man, which may be where I got my own shyness, although some friends do not see me as shy, and I have enjoyed talking to audiences of a thousand in Chicago and Madrid. But I listened intently at the dinner table when he spoke of something that had come up in the office. He was a link to the outside world, in particular the world of business—no matter that he did not make a great deal of money. More important, he was a proud and caring father.

We were among the earliest in Hastings House and all of Hastings to have a television set—a Magnavox with a built-in 33 rpm vinyl record player encased in a mahogany furniture piece. One day, my father came home from the city with a recording of arias from *Aida*, one sung by Beniamino Gigli and the other by an Italian soprano. I think he, a Nelson Eddy fan, wanted to acquaint me with singers. He also supported my own musical endeavors.

Sometime after I took up the trumpet, he brought home a recording of bugle calls performed by Harry Glantz, preferred principal trumpet of Arturo Toscanini and idol of William Vacchiano (more on him later). The support I felt from my father meant a great deal to me.

We all took pleasure in several family rituals: the summer trips in our 1939 Chrysler back to Chicago and Mason City to see relatives—my twenty-six cousins—and, later, the annual vacation on Prince Edward Island in the Gulf of Saint Lawrence. My father and I played golf, although I was never any good at it. Turkey dinner on Thanksgiving was another precious ritual. So was Christmas with the ceremony of going into town with my father to select a tree and decorating it with beautiful ornaments from as far away as Prague and a sparing amount of tinsel.

My mother went all-out with Christmas dinner at midday after the handing out of presents under the tree.

At age thirteen or so, my parents introduced me to Protestantism; my father and I would stand side by side, singing some of the great hymns of Luther and others. They seemed not to care that I eventually didn't continue churchgoing.

Looking back, I see that my parents generally let me be pretty free to explore and test myself. They didn't object to my taking a six-hour bicycle ride up and down Route 9, a truck route with no lack of traffic. They didn't disapprove of my working poolside at a country club to earn some money with which to buy a car. I think their trusting and easy-going parenting helped me find my way to a richly rewarding life.

In high school, much of my free time was devoted to music— I got to play trumpet in the high school orchestra and concert band. In the ninth grade, my idol was the first chair trumpet player, Charles Norris, who graduated that spring and played in the Charlie Barnett Band that summer. I was delighted to be his replacement as first trumpet in the high school, and I went on to play in the Hudson Valley Symphony Orchestra, the Amherst College Concert Band, and the Smith College Orchestra.

When Charlie graduated, so did the members of the dance band he played in, which opened an opportunity for some of us to start a new band. Our first gig was across the river in Nyack, and we went on to play all over southern Westchester County. This was a lot of fun, and we made some money. I particularly enjoyed playing a solo in "Stella by Starlight," trying to keep in my head the sound of Billy Butterfield when he was with the Artie Shaw Band.

Learning to play well required, as the old joke has it, "practice, practice, practice." My trumpet teacher, Melvin Warshaw—a student of the great William Vacchiano, principal trumpet of the

New York Philharmonic—had come out of Julliard. So I found myself often listening to Vacchiano leading the brass section in Robert Shaw's recording of Bach's B-Minor Mass. My high school music director, Howard Marsh (or Howie), was a singer in the choir on that recording. A few years later, I happened to hear for the first time Roger Voisin, finally becoming principal trumpet of the Boston Symphony Orchestra, in a chilling rendition of "The Trumpet Shall Sound" in Handel's *Messiah*. The sound was palpable. It may well be that these youthful heroes of mine—Vacchiano and Voisin—set examples of what performance could be and what creativity can lead to.

In a bit of luck, Howie got permission to give a small class for about eight of us in musicology. One day he gave us some homework: to harmonize a C-major scale by putting a succession of chords under it. What I conceived surprised me and Howie, too. I sensed that I possessed some creativity—as, I later realized, a multitude of people do.

Meeting a number of Nobel winners in Stockholm decades later, I was struck by how many of them were accomplished musicians. It could very well be that people who have talent in theorizing and testing in science also have some talent at expression in the arts. This reminds me that once I was out of graduate school and hoping to catch up a little with my reading, I found myself reading five or six of C. P. Snow's novels. Looking back, I found these novels have the same theme: creativity in the arts and creativity in the sciences derive from a common core—the creativity of people.

In late summer 1951, it was time to leave home and go to college. I entered Amherst College, a men's college beautifully situated in the Pioneer Valley of western Massachusetts. About three hundred students were enrolled in the freshman class—the class of 1955.

All of us, I think, felt privileged to be there. On the Commons, surrounded by buildings some three centuries old, students sometimes played frisbee on the lawn in front of the library. The administrative offices and Johnson Chapel were on the west side as were the two original dormitories, North College and South College. I lived in the latter over freshman year, as did most of the classmates I became close to.

This first year was challenging. The English course started with a map and the question "what is Amherst?" When someone answered, "It's the dot labeled 'Amherst' on the map," I realized that some in my class were more sophisticated than I was—in some dimensions, at any rate. I took required courses in a foreign language, calculus, and the sciences and completed physical tests, such as pull-ups and swimming. Each morning we had to be in the nondenominational Johnson Chapel for a sermon. I sensed that we were being trained to be able to play important roles in the country. All of this was a bit daunting.

The two-semester course in the humanities would help shape my outlook on life and my life's work. The ancient Greek plays and the ancient Roman sages impressed me and so did the works of the Renaissance. I was thunderstruck by the ambitiousness of Cellini, who murdered a rival. We read Homer's *Odyssey* on exploration, Erasmus on expanding possibilities, Luther on individualism, Montaigne's essays on personal growth, Cervantes's *Don Quixote* on the need to test oneself, and Shakespeare's *Hamlet* on the courage to act.

A lecture course on Plato, David Hume, and Henri Bergson also left a mark on me. I was stunned at the beauty of Plato's dialogues, the importance of Hume's imaging the new, and Bergson's notions of creativity and becoming, each of which came to be more and more a part of my work over the last quarter of a century.

These and other great figures of the past have continued to have an influence on me—particularly, their boldness and their originality. We need to have these examples to stir us if we are to strike out in a new direction.

Exposure to other cultures is also important for one's intellectual development—for broadening the mind and having experiences one would not have otherwise imagined. Two classmates, Richard Davis and John Stone, invited me to join them in the summer for a grand tour of Europe, the short version. It was just seven years since the war's end, and it was fascinating to gain a sense of the Europe of normal times. After some days on the Atlantic and an hour on the train, we were in Paris drinking beer on a starlit night in the Place de l'Opéra. Soon after we were in Rome, dining on a rooftop in Parioli, and then in Vienna at the State Opera House. Last, we traveled to London and Oxford. I cannot forget another experience: On the way back from Vienna, the night train paused somewhere outside of Munich. Outside was a vast field of rubble as far as the eye could see—a shocking sight of the war I had not been in. I felt I had become more a person of the world.

At Amherst, first in the South College dorm and then in the Jeff Club (an alternative to the fraternities), I was fortunate, as in my earlier schooling in Hastings, to have friends who went on to accomplish things—to make a mark. Robert Fagles, who immersed himself in classical literature, reached the forefront in the wave of new English translations of both the *Iliad* and the *Odyssey*. Michael Sahl, the most brilliant among us and already a composer and pianist, delighted us with bluegrass songs played on a five-string banjo and the occasional performance of Bach's Brandenburg Concerto No. 5 on the barroom piano (thumbtacks on the hammers); he became a known figure in the music world. Ralph Allen, who could memorize every book and write exam answers with unprecedented speed, realized his ambition to be a playwright with his Broadway hit *Sugar Babies*. What talent and ambition. So, the Jeff Club was special. When Robert Frost made one of his occasional visits to Amherst, he came around to the Jeff Club and spoke to the rapt audience. We all knew the line, "I took the [road] less traveled by, and that has made all the difference," from Frost's poem, "The Road Not Taken." I am sure that all this inspired me and challenged me.

I was beginning to think I would major in philosophy—I found it intriguing and clear—when my father asked me to take a course in economics, thinking that I would like it. I enrolled in the introductory course in my second year, and found my father was right. Almost immediately, I found the brilliant textbook by Paul Samuelson and the witty lectures by James Nelson (a friend of Paul's from Harvard graduate school) were engrossing and fun, too. I took additional courses in the subject and decided to major in economics.

In part, I was drawn to the field in hopes of getting the answer to a puzzle I saw in the introductory course. It was not clear to me how *macroeconomics* (which is about the determination of aggregates, such as investment and saving, labor force, unemployment, and interest rates) might be connected to *microeconomics* (which is all about the behavior of individual firms, workers, and investors). There seemed to be a disconnect between the two fields. No doubt, I was also drawn by the sense that bridging the gap might make a difference for economic policy.

It was yet another piece of good luck that a teacher of mine in my junior and senior years was Arnold Collery, a young economist out of Princeton, with a razor-sharp mind who worked in the area of macroeconomics from monetary theory to business cycle models. It so happened that years later he was applying to be dean of Columbia College, where he had a hand in converting the College to a co-ed institution, and I had the satisfaction of recommending him for the position. Later, we became colleagues in Columbia's economics department.

Toward the end of my junior year, the Economics Department announced a lecture by Paul Samuelson, whom I knew of as the author of the textbook I studied and, in those years, the leading figure in economic theory. On top of that, he was going to interview me and two or three other top students in the department. This was awesome, to be sure. I had seen him in a debate with Arnold Toynbee on CBS-TV and realized then that his brilliance must have been unsurpassed in his time.

His lecture on Austrian economics was impressive. I may have been nervous about the interview, but he put me at ease. He said that whatever graduate school I chose, it would be valuable to stay there as long as I could because afterward there would be many demands on my time. In any case, I felt almost as if I had made a new friend, and it proved to be the start of a very long friendship. I recall that at the end, when I spoke with him over the phone in autumn 2009, he commented that he was ninety-four and no longer up to smiling at people after giving a talk.

Not all of what I learned came from the formality of books, articles, and lectures. In my senior year, I found in the stacks of Amherst's library the sharp exchanges between John Maynard Keynes and Friedrich Hayek over the effects of what would be called fiscal stimulus and monetary stimulus. I was excited to see that economic journals—or one of them at one time, at any rate—was hospitable to new thinking, and I was delighted to see the people behind the theories.

It was around this time that Willard L. Thorp, a towering figure by any measure, rejoined Amherst after several years working as an economist and statistician on Wall Street, chairing the Temporary National Economic Commission (TNEC) on monopoly in the Roosevelt administration and, after the war, serving as right hand of William Clayton, "catalyst of the Marshall Plan," in the State Department.[1] Thorp proceeded to create Amherst's Merrill Center for Economics. The first annual conference was held that summer in the Charles Merrill estate in Southampton, Long Island, and I was one of four students invited to help.

Those two weeks were full of experiences. It was an opportunity to meet many of the leading economists of that time—Gottfried Haberler, Jacob Viner, and Aaron Gordon among others. But some more personal moments remain deep in my mind. I had only recently read of General Lucius Clay in the *New Yorker*, which called him the most important person in the nation, and there he was in front of me at the reception area of the mansion, engaging me in conversation. (He asked me what kind of career I wanted. I replied, government, though, in fact, I had only brief positions in the public sector.) There was Clarice Thorp, Willard's fiercely devoted wife, who ran the operation. I was struck by her sharp mind, and she appeared to have high expectations for me, which gave me encouragement. I was fortunate to get to know Emile Despres, a wonderful man of wide experience and generosity, who participated in the event. He took an interest in us and regaled us four with his stories. He and I talked about Sloan Wilson's *The Man in the Gray Flannel Suit* in which the main character, Tom Rath, struggles to find happiness in a material culture—my first conversation on the experience of work. It was also the first discussion I had heard on the subject of job satisfaction. More than a decade later, I wrote about the importance to a person of having work that is engaging and, in recent years, I have written about a long decline of job satisfaction.

On entering my senior year, I decided to go to graduate school. In a senior seminar, Collery was taking us through the business cycle models of that era, 1900 to 1950, which fortified my decision. What had sparked my interest in doing graduate work was my curiosity to get to the bottom of the "disconnect" between the microeconomics of wage and price setting on the one hand, and the prevailing macroeconomic models of employment, price level, and their fluctuations on the other. To do that, I felt, I would need to enter the foundations of economic theory, which I supposed would be central to graduate study in the great universities.

I applied to the Massachusetts Institute of Technology, having in mind the brilliance of Samuelson and Solow; to Harvard, thinking of its enormous prestige; and to Yale, about which I knew rather little. Helped by letters of support from Nelson and Collery, all three accepted me. I gathered that Yale's economics department had become hugely cosmopolitan and strikingly diverse in its views. It also offered the best fellowship, so I opted for Yale.

I was never in doubt that I would not have had this opportunity without Amherst—the profound education there and the personal support of Jim and Arnold helped prepare me for graduate school. I saw Amherst as having become an even better place for students' education and personal development when in 1975 it opened its admissions to women. Later, however, I was dismayed to learn that the college dropped the two-semester humanities course that I had come to believe was essential to my intellectual growth.

Yale did not disappoint. The Gothic structures on the main campus were inspiring. The nearby town of New Haven had some amenities: a good restaurant offering Austro-Hungarian cuisine and a theater that was a regular stopover for tryouts of plays headed for Broadway (but it was no New York). In my first year there, 1955–56, I thoroughly enjoyed the two-semester course on the foundations of economic theory given by William Fellner, the wide-ranging course on international trade by Thomas Schelling, the expert course on the international monetary system by Robert Triffin, a course on monetary policy given by Henry Wallich, the course on general equilibrium theory given by Tjalling Koopmans, a basic introduction to statistics given by Robert Summers, and—though it was not my cup of tea—the advanced course in statistics by James Tobin, who later generously gave me a reading course in macroeconomic models and from whom I learned the importance of investigating the degree of empirical support for the models we dream up. I had many interactions with Arthur Okun and some contact with Gérard Debreu and Jacob Marshak—all in Yale's Cowles Foundation for Research in Economics. In my view, Yale's department had the most impressive roster of economists since the so-called Cambridge Circus from 1925 to 1935 built around Keynes—though Chicago was strong, too, with Milton Friedman, George Stigler, Gary Becker, Harry Johnson, T. W. Schultz, Ronald Coase, and Lloyd Metzler. In general, the Yale department was quite intellectual.

Some of the teachers had interesting lives.[2] Tobin, like some of the others, was extremely smart. Herman Wouk's novel, *The Caine Mutiny*, tells—based on a real-life event in Tobin's life—of the time when a ship became becalmed by an engine failure (thus a sitting duck for submarine torpedoes), and midshipman Tobit, after hours of studying the unfamiliar technical data, is able to restart the engine.

By far the most energetic lecturer was Robert Summers, father of Larry and brother-in-law of Kenneth Arrow. In his elementary statistics class, he quoted a student, possibly imaginary, who interrupted the lecturer to exclaim, "But sir! Where are the people in that model?" I realized that the student had been expecting to find in the models his perception of people doing such things as forming expectations or conceiving new methods. In the course of the modeling I was to do, that story, possibly apocryphal, often came to mind.

What Yale had to offer was not only its outstanding faculty members. The university frequently received many scholars and intellectuals on book tours or on their way to New York or Washington, DC. I had less time to hear these lectures than I would have liked, but I was fascinated to hear the novelist and scientist C. P. Snow lecturing on the regrettable division between science and art. Snow believed, and I would come to agree, that this division was a serious obstacle to addressing the world's problems. After I graduated, I read his book *Corridors of Power* and went on to read several more in the Strangers and Brothers series. I have come to think that I was curious about the lives of creative people in both the sciences and the arts.

I also encountered outstanding students from the past. I was reading the *New York Times* in the Reading Room of the Hall of Graduate Studies after lunch when I looked up to see towering above me Dean Acheson, the secretary of state in the Truman administration and one of the most well-known and admired figures in the country. (Years later, at the commencement ceremony in which I received my doctorate, he led the procession, wrapped in a brilliant red gown and caring a silver scepter.) He remarked that hardly any students read the papers anymore, which plainly worried him. I agreed.

Then, taking up communism, he referred to the critics who scorned the argument for Soviet communism on the ground that the end justifies the means. "What else could justify the means?" he remarked. I could only nod by way of agreeing with his criticism. After years of pondering over this comment, I concluded he had in mind that communism would be justified *if* it were the only means or the best means to, say, equality, and we cared *only* about equality. Although many people in Western societies do want to see Rawls's wage justice for the least advantaged, Gunnar Myrdal's interracial justice, and Betty Friedan's intergender justice (even if more justice might do little to reduce inequality), most people in the West also need an economy in which jobs are engaging and even interesting—thus offering a life of richness. Communism (socialism) and corporatism (fascism) do not meet these diverse needs.

The diversity of opinion in the department was a joy. I vaguely recall that in a poll that Henry Wallich took on some issue over which there was considerable division, Tobin and Okun were strongly Keynesian, without being rabid, while Fellner was not; nor did Triffin and Wallich show much confidence or even interest in Keynesianism. Yet there was a great deal of warmth and respect between Fellner and Tobin. My views did not evolve very far in these four years. I am sure I thought that monetary stimulus was effective medicine to hasten recovery from a recession, while worrying that fiscal stimulus might weigh on investment. But that was a question I was to turn to more than once in my career.

My third year was an opportunity for research and maybe an early dissertation—I had no classwork and still no teaching to do. But I didn't have a single idea in my head of what topic to make the subject of my doctoral dissertation. Two years of mostly methods and models had distracted me from what I had wanted to do in deciding to become an economic theorist. When I asked Tom Schelling for an idea, he suggested a reconstruction of the theory of national saving to allow for overlapping generations—a topic that Roy Harrod and Jan de Van Graaf had mentioned, and Franco Modigliani was to succeed in understanding with his work in 1961. I utterly failed with that project and had to drop it, having lost a year. I hadn't learned the necessity of keeping things simple, at least at the start. This was frustrating, but it didn't hold me back.

Looking back, it occurs to me that in these difficult years in college and graduate school—the 1950s—I like many others needed the diversion of the movies, especially in that period. That decade experienced an explosion of new kinds of films in Stockholm with Bergman, especially *Sawdust and Tinsel* and *Wild Strawberries*, in Paris with its Nouvelle Vague, and in Hollywood with the brilliant, technicolor movies that remain fixtures in my mind to this day. This explosion of creativity was impressive, and it broadened my sense of humanity.

In the fourth year, things turned up. Although I did not at first have a dissertation underway, I began teaching my first course: an introduction to economics for freshmen in the fall semester of 1957–58. It seemed to go well enough, but student evaluations had not yet started, so it was hard to tell.

A sample of student opinion came thirty-nine years later. Paul Steiger, then the managing editor of the *Wall Street Journal* and later the founder of ProPublica, phoned me to say that he wanted to organize a luncheon in my honor at the *Journal*. After a date had been set, I asked him whether we knew each other.

He said, "Yes, you were my teacher in the introductory economics course I took at Yale." With some trepidation, I asked him how it went.

"You were great," he said.

Incredulous, I replied, "Really?"

"Yes, you were excellent. And it was your course that led me to change my major from political science to economics." Curious, I asked him how that ended up.

"Not well," he said. "You were the only good teacher I had in economics until the senior seminar given by James Tobin." I didn't know what to say.

When I mentioned to Jim Tobin that I still didn't have a thesis topic, he had a thought. He suggested I figure out a way to measure how much of an observed inflation is cost-push and how much is demand-pull. This exercise in model building and application to data went very well. At last, I had something to show.[3] On a beautiful June day, I received my doctorate.

1

BEGINNING MY CAREER
Golden Rule of Saving and Public Debt

Afew days after Yale commencement, I flew to Los Angeles to take a position at the RAND Corporation in Santa Monica, California, which had emerged as an important place for talented experts in economics, mathematics, operations research, and other fields to work on problems of importance for national defense. The financing came largely from the U.S. Air Force and, it would appear, the State Department. Unexpectedly, Thomas Schelling was there—on his way to figuring out a way to put a stop to the Cold War. Kenneth Arrow, already a top economic theorist whom I got to know through Robert Summers, was busy at work, as was Richard Bellman, the mathematician who had just made a breakthrough in optimization over time. A team of theorists was also doing new work on "technical progress," more specifically, innovation, led by Richard Nelson. After lunch, we often strolled on the boardwalk along the beach, exchanging ideas and arguing. What an exciting place it was.

It was also a thrill to be in Los Angeles. Up Wilshire Boulevard, automobile showrooms were gleaming with Aston Martins and Bentleys and furniture showrooms rich with chairs by Hans Wegner and Barcelona. New pop singers were getting their start at the Troubadour on North Santa Monica Boulevard. (The peak came in the 1970s with such greats as Elton John, Neil Young, Carole King, Carly Simon, and James Taylor.) Innumerable movie theaters were spread across the county. There was also an opera house and a great art museum, and a concert hall was coming fairly soon. The atmosphere of California was a sight to behold—Malibu, Bel Air, Beverly Hills, the beaches, and pools—much of which is captured in the paintings of David Hockney, who arrived there in 1964.

It was fun to travel around California and meet some people outside Los Angeles. One weekend, Harvey Wagner, an operation research expert at RAND and Stanford, took me up to Berkeley where I met contemporaries, notably Dale Jorgenson, with whom I would intersect many times in our careers, and—most impressive—Amartya Sen with whom I have been keeping in touch ever since. He has set a standard of seriousness and rigor I have tried to meet over my career.

My work at RAND was engaging enough. The opening I was offered was in the Logistic Department, where there were several economists and statisticians. I worked generally every week, Monday to Thursday, on a somewhat challenging problem involving the stock of airplane parts ready for use and the stock of parts requiring repair. When I had solved the problem, Ken Arrow commented that it was one of the rare examples of a solution to a two-dimensional problem in dynamic programming. (He tried to squeeze it into a book he was editing but it was too late, and I lost interest in it.) On Fridays I worked on the problem I had set myself: a nation's optimal accumulation of risky capital—a project I completed later. Months later I showed my equations to Richard Bellman, celebrated originator of what he dubbed dynamic programming. I was uncertain what he would say.

"This is trivial!" he said. "The capital stock goes to infinity."

"Yes," I said, "but I'm studying *how fast* it goes!"

RAND was great fun, but ultimately, I felt the need to rejoin academia to do whatever basic research in economic theory I would prove capable of doing. I was offered a position of assistant professor at Yale's Cowles Foundation for Research in Economics with reduced teaching. Nothing comparable was available. So, I went back east to try to restart my career as an economic theorist.

In September 1960 and back at Yale, I started out with little idea of what theoretical work I could do over the ensuing six years and, of course, had no idea at all of what success or failure might result—I would experience both, as it turned out. Absent any new theory of my own to work on, I began keeping my eye out for any unnoticed implication or room for improvement in existing theory.

Theorists thrive on their articles in academic or scientific journals. Of the three such papers I published while I was at Cowles, the first and most widely read was "The Golden Rule of Accumulation," which appeared in the short papers section of the *American Economic Review* in September 1961.[1] The idea—drawn on the 1950s growth models built by Robert Solow and Trevor Swan—is simple enough.[2] Suppose the world has long enjoyed technical progress at a constant rate and will do so for a long time. Suppose also that the proportion of income society chooses to save (the "saving rate" for short) is going to be constant, the *level* of which could be too high as well as too low. As I showed with a little math, the level that would sustain indefinitely the *highest* growth path of consumption turns out to be equal to the percentage share of income going to profits (rather than wages). That would drive the rate of return on capital toward the rate of growth of the national income. This abstracted radically from many things. But it showed that (as a logical matter) there can be *too much* saving. That finding may also have put into question the contention among some planners that a huge increase in the saving ratio could avert the fall of per capita consumption that would otherwise result from the steep rise of the world's population. (Of greater concern than the downward pressure on the growth path of consumption is the environmental damage of endlessly rising population.)

This short paper has always occupied a strange position in my work in economic theory. I set out the mathematical model in the setting of townsfolk rapt in the excitement of the equations being unfolded. Some readers expressed amusement—Robert Solow wrote a sequel fable though he did not publish it—while others were not comfortable with it. Some people have asked me why I took that approach. Maybe it was to gain attention to the problem and its solution. Maybe it was to amuse readers and myself. Maybe it was to satirize the extreme simplicity of economists' models, in which we abstract from so much. And maybe it reflected a need I felt to express a little imagination—to exercise whatever creativity I possessed. Another oddity is that, while many authors of economic papers wait years for any citation of their work, this short paper leaped onto the pages of textbooks and journal articles within months. Later, the Nobel Prize committee judged the "Golden Rule" paper notable enough to cite it in their four-page announcement of my award.

The second paper of mine in those years at Cowles was "The Accumulation of Risky Capital," published in *Econometrica* in October 1962.[3] I had started it at RAND and had completed it at Cowles. It arose out of a curiosity to analyze whether increased riskiness in the rate of return to investment tended to *shrink* the supply of saving, thus squeezing investment (under equilibrium conditions) and slowing the accumulation of capital or instead tended to *expand* the supply of saving (as risk-averse investors felt more vulnerable and motivated to hold larger cushions), thus opening the room for more investment and thus speeding up capital accumulation. The answer was that it could go either way. (This result may help to explain why households that depend primarily upon risky capital income, such as farmers or wealthy heirs, are comparatively thrifty.) Although I wasn't impelled to go farther in this area, I was pleased to see it was extended by Paul Samuelson in a 1969 paper and built on by others at Harvard Business School.

The third paper I conceived while at Cowles was "The New View of Investment," published by Harvard's *Quarterly Journal of Economics* in November 1962.[4] Following his pioneering "growth model" in the 1950s, Solow took up the concept of technological advances that have to be "embodied" in new capital goods to be productive. "In the new view," as I put it, "the role of investment is to modernize as well as deepen the capital stock." I found that in the long run, injecting embodied technical progress into the growth model made no difference. The growth rate and the rate of return on investment are shown to be independent of the degree to which technical advances must be "embodied" in investment. I also studied the short-run dynamics in this model. For example, an anticipated rise in the labor force growth rate leads to a more modern capital stock, given the investment-output ratio. Although the paper was well done and not uninteresting, it was not seminal and did not draw much interest.

It was during my time at Cowles that I would feel closer to the world that my colleagues and I would be addressing in our work. In my first year (1960–1961) there, John F. Kennedy won the presidential contest with Richard Nixon and took office in January 1961. I will never forget that day: I was notified I would have to proctor a final exam at Woolsey Hall, more than a mile from where I lived. On my walk there, it was snowing, so when the exam ended, I was in a rush to get home to see Kennedy and Robert Frost, whom I had been thrilled to meet at Amherst, speak at the inauguration. The sidewalks were so deep in snow and the icy wind so fierce, however, that by the time I got home, the inauguration was over. I had missed Kennedy's speech and Frost's presentation.[5]

The Kennedy administration, replacing that of Dwight Eisenhower, drew upon a new roster of economists. James Tobin went to Washington for a year at the Council of Economic Advisers, and Arthur Okun took his place the next year. In a way, this marked the importance that Yale had acquired. Yet, around the same time, Schelling had moved to Harvard—a huge loss—and some of the star figures at Cowles who had come from Chicago left: Gérard Debreu to the University of California and Jacob Marschak to UCLA.

A little later, Solow, who was based at the Massachusetts Institute of Technology (MIT), was called to help at the Council, which left the department short-handed. I was invited to be a visiting associate professor at MIT in 1962–1963 to replace Bob in one or two of his courses, including a challenging seminar for doctoral students on capital theory in the fall semester. In that seminar, with the course outline and reading list presented to me, I had to read and teach material that was often unfamiliar and sometimes difficult—with Bob sometimes dropping in. Moreover, the students were all extremely smart, such as Christian von Weizsäcker, Michael Intriligator, David Levhari, and Eytan Sheshinski. But it felt good to prove to myself that I could do it well enough.

Yet I, like the majority of my fellow academics, did not go into my profession to teach. I went into academics to have the support needed to do research and to write books and articles. Most of us want in our work to contribute to society and to the world. We need to keep our teaching up to par for any number of opportunities: to interact with and guide gifted students or to share our theories and findings.

At MIT, I came to see how brilliant and insightful the stars of the Economics Department were in those times and became aware of how fertile the department had been since the early 1950s. There were not only the superstars—Samuelson, Solow, and Franco Modigliani—but also leaders in their fields, such as Charles Kindleberger in history, Evsey Domar in development, and Francis Bator in public economics. I enjoyed the opportunity to engage with them and broaden my sense of what others were striving toward.

Above all, it was a joy to have so much contact with Paul Samuelson. At a cocktail party in his home in Belmont, he introduced me to some of the people of Harvard, and at a delightful dinner at my place near Harvard Square, he sang a line from "The Marriage of Figaro." Paul was very widely read. Someone said he read a book every night—perhaps to get away for some hours from the economic questions on his mind during the day. The breadth of his interests, cultural and historical, helps to explain the breadth of his textbook and our rapport. We had exchanges about economics, although not as many as I would have liked. A table in the faculty dining room was the site of many hypotheses and arguments. After I voiced a thought on some matter, Paul proceeded to question that idea at some length. Francis Bator, sitting somewhere between us, asked Paul whether he didn't think he should let up; but Paul, pointing out that I was taking it well, persisted with his interrogation. I remember fondly those lunches at MIT. We often underestimate the importance of such interchanges as tests of our ideas.

In the spring, with much less teaching to do, I began work on a new project on public debt. I might have hesitated to do it, with its analytical challenges and controversial issues, but when McGraw-Hill asked me to produce a monograph on the subject, I plunged into that mire in late June.

BACKGROUND: CONTROVERSY OVER PUBLIC DEBT

Public debt has always been a subject of radically differing views. In the view sometimes called "crude Keynesianism," the public debt that builds up when conditions force a government to undertake massive deficit spending is not a problem: The cost to the public of paying the additional taxes needed to pay the interest on the debt is offset by the additional interest income the public receives from its holdings of the public debt. "We owe the debt to ourselves," as many Keynesians liked to say—and Jim Tobin said to me in person. In other words: "We, a self-governing people, are (in a sense) the borrowers and, in the aggregate, also the lenders." But that is a truism. It is not a theoretical model implying that the public debt is harmless nor a statistical model showing that public debt has no effect.

The many Keynesians who hold this belief generally oppose policies to restrain government spending or raise tax rates to reduce a debt level that has ballooned or to curb its rise. In recent years, they have derided such policies as a symptom of a compulsive desire for "austerity" in some Western nations. But this position reduces to absurdity: If it were true that any and all of the government's spending could be costlessly debt-financed rather than tax-financed, there would be no taxing at all—only borrowing.

In the real world, when tax rates are raised to pay the interest on the debt—that is, to service the debt—the taxpayers face not only the so-called burden when writing the check but also the "excess burden." The cost to the country's taxpayers leads them to cut back their work and their saving in an effort to escape some of the resulting burden, which then forces the government to raise tax rates some more, and so on until the taxpayers quit the game. The resulting fall of after-tax wage rates and interest rates brings a loss of national income and ultimately national wealth.[6]

Other economists, though, see little harm in the high public debt levels that have emerged in the past—with World War II and the 2008 Global Financial Crisis—and has emerged again with the tax cuts followed by coronavirus spending on the grounds that the public debt now is not *seriously* burdensome since the inflation-adjusted real interest rate on debt in general— the famous r in macroeconomics—has been extraordinarily low for several years. But an increased public debt does drive a *wedge* between wealth and capital, thus causing the capital stock to be less than it would have otherwise been and causing real wages to grow less high than they would have otherwise done. Moreover, to expect r to stay so extremely low in the decades to come may turn out not to be right.

Some other economists have long seen no serious harm in the public debt on the belief that nations still experiencing technological progress and a degree of population growth can reasonably expect to "grow out of" its debt. But if the growth rate of productivity—the famous g in macroeconomics—is going to remain as sluggish as it has largely been since the early 1970s, then even such a nation will not perceptibly "grow out of" its public debt for decades.

A deeper point has long concerned neoclassical economists. If over the period of large-scale government borrowing, the public has cut back purchases of consumer goods to buy the government's sales of bonds, their wealth will be *increased* at the end of this period, although the nation's capital stock will not be—not appreciably, at any rate. If instead the public has cut back purchases of new issues of company shares to buy the government's sales of bonds, the nation's capital will be *decreased*, although wealth will not be. Either way, government debt introduces a wedge between wealth and capital.

The effects of that "wedge" have long been a topic of economics. Neoclassical economics predicts that an enlargement of the public debt increases wealth and thus boosts consumption and squeezes investment. In neoclassical theory, this results in a slowdown of capital accumulation and productivity growth. History appears to confirm that. Over the four years of World War II ending in 1945, the United States accumulated a massive public debt. This was followed by booming consumption from 1946 to 1948 yet *reduced* levels of the investment-output ratio in the same period. World War I was shorter, ending in 1918, but was followed by the 1918 flu epidemic. Although the United States was not heavily engaged in this war, it nevertheless exhibited a markedly low investment-output ratio after the flu epidemic from 1921 to 1923.[7]

In 1817, David Ricardo, a founder of classical economics, had the thought that public debt tends to "blind us to our real situation" and thus to "make us less thrifty."[8] In this thinking, paper wealth is a drug of sorts: In stimulating consumption demand, it squeezes investment, thus slowing the growth of the capital stock and the growth of the supply of consumer goods.

In the 1960s, Ricardo's idea was developed further.[9] Modigliani, a neoclassical economist, built a model in which the wedge between wealth and capital created by the public debt is a drag on capital accumulation: the path of capital is tilted down toward a new steady-growth state with reduced capital.[10] With this study and others, the idea of keeping the public debt small to buttress saving, and thus capital formation, became a tenet of neoclassical thought.

But does neoclassical theory imply that a zero level of public debt is best? Is this better than maintaining the debt? And if the debt is maintained, would a tax policy offset the debt's effects so that the mix of debt and taxes would be neutral—that is, neutral for consumption and work, and thus for investment and growth? These matters and more were taken up in *Fiscal Neutrality Toward Economic Growth*, my first book-length exploration into a branch of economic theory and policy.[11]

NEUTRALIZING THE PUBLIC DEBT?

Fiscal Neutrality begins with an investigation of the simplest portrait of an economy—the standard macro model of a closed economy producing just one good, which is where theorists typically start. (Think of Defoe's *Robinson Crusoe*, Smith's *Wealth of Nations*, or Keynes's *General Theory*.)

The question addressed first in this setting is whether a government debt that has emerged, with its wealth effects on the supply of labor and the supply of saving, might be *neutralized* in this economy. The answer is only to a degree:

> By levying the appropriate amount of net lump-sum taxes the government can raise present plus expected future taxes so as to . . . neutralize the incidence of the debt. . . . [This] neutralization is possible because the tax has only a wealth (or net-worth) effect on

consumption demand and labor supply. The same tax which neutralizes the impact of the debt upon consumption demand will also neutralize the impact of the debt upon labor supply.[12]

But a lump-sum tax, in falling on low- and high-income earners alike, would be viewed as unfair.

Is it the case that, with only *non*-lump-sum taxes remaining, the debt can still be neutralized? The answer is no:

> [An] expenditure tax cannot simultaneously neutralize the impacts . . . on both consumption demand and labor supply. . . . If the impact of the debt on consumption demand is neutralized, [requiring a restoration of wealth,] the impact of the debt on labor supply [,which depends on wage rates as well as wealth,] cannot be.[13]

Conversely, if the *supply of labor* is neutralized, the impact on *consumption demand* cannot be.

A more complicated argument in the book shows that an income tax cannot neutralize government debt. The complication is that both the interest rate, which is relevant to consumption demand, and the wage rate, which is relevant to labor supply, are affected by the income tax rate. "It will be an accident if the same tax rate which would neutralize the debt's impact upon consumption demand would also neutralize the debt's impact on labor supply. Hence, it is not *generally* possible exactly to neutralize a positive initial government debt by means of an income tax."[14]

To summarize: Public debt, in adding to wealth—in the normal case, at any rate—*contracts investment*, thus shrinking the capital stock, slowing the rise of wage rates and lifting real interest rates, although the capital stock does not decrease as much as the debt increases. (Modigliani's different model yielded the same result.)

It is often said that this theory would apply only to public debt that was issued to finance the services provided by the public sector from national defense to public health. I recall this issue came up on a flight back to the East Coast from a conference put on by Modigliani in Athens in the late 1970s. Sitting across the aisle from Tobin and the brilliant Pentti Kouri, the Finnish economic theorist who focused on international macroeconomics, I must have said something about public debt crowding out investment, for Tobin said public debt that financed government investment projects does *not* set back the accumulation of the capital in the private sector, which is a tenet of standard macroeconomics. I wondered about that—having in mind that the deficit spending displaces either some saving or some investing, thus creating a wedge between wealth and capital. Tobin took out his pencil. We landed without having resolved the matter.

I have stuck here to the settings studied in *Fiscal Neutrality*. Of course, public-debt financing of government projects, the costs of which are expected to be covered in the future by user charges, does not set back investment. But deficit financing of *all other* public expenditure does.[15]

TESTING THE KEYNESIAN VIEW

Which view appears to be most nearly right? The Keynesian view that public debt serves to pull up employment, thus reducing the unemployment rate and inducing higher participation? Or the neoclassical view that public debt sets the capital stock onto a lower path, thus decreasing the labor force and employment? (There is also the "neo-Keynesian" view, that public debt financing government *investment* may dampen *or* advance the capital stock in the business sector, so that the public debt may matter little.)

Some years later, statistical estimates of the effect of public debt first appeared in the 1980s and then a broader study appeared in the 1990s book *Structural Slumps*.[16] A finding there, drawn from a study of 18 countries, was that an increase of the "world public debt" led to an increase of the unemployment rate. Another finding was that the world debt increases unemployment by pushing up the world real interest rate. The implications for the world capital stock were not studied.

On a seemingly quite different matter, I began in 2018 to investigate a central post-Keynesian tenet: whether among the dozen countries studied, the ones that injected the larger fiscal stimulus into the economy following the 2008–2010 recession were also the ones with the fastest rate of recovery in 2011–2017.[17] The findings were negative. Fiscal stimulus was evidently not measurably stimulating. We may surmise from these results that, in particular, investment did not respond to the fiscal stimulus as well as expenditure in general.

Now, an ongoing exploration by Gylfi Zoega, Hian Teck Hoon, and myself of the G–7 countries from 1960 to 2019 finds that a nation's so-called employment rate—that is, $1 - u$, where u is the unemployment rate—is *decreased* by public debt. In the theoretical model underlying the estimated equation, the public debt acts, in pushing up the real rate of interest, to contract investment activity and thus to lower wages and employment to lower paths. We also find negative effects of government borrowing on lending for investment and on saving for future consumption.

In view of these latter findings, it ought not to puzzle us that the nations deploying the "stimulus" of deficit spending did not recover faster than the others. True, it has come to be common sense that a tax cut encourages consumption spending. However, as the years went by, the reduced tax rates on top of increased annual spending brought elevated fiscal deficits—despite any private forces acting to reduce the deficit. So, the public debt surged above its trend growth path, while the doughty fiscal deficit carried on.

At the present stage of macroeconomic research, it appears safe to infer that the public debt, when quite large, is a significant force dragging capital and wage rates to lower growth paths and that deficit spending is best not counted on to boost consumption or investment when the public debt is at significant heights.

It does not follow that post-Keynesian economics is to be consigned to the ash heap. But I think it would be right to say that post-Keynesian theory is just one viewpoint—one worth consulting only alongside the assemblage of macroeconomic perspectives from the neoclassical to the more modern.

Fiscal Neutrality did not gain wide interest at all, but it did give me the confidence to think that I would likely engage in more book-length model building and statistical testing. The bit of creativity I used in building a theoretical structure for use in the book's analysis and in building more such structures for the purposes of analysis may have been important decades later when I was thinking—or at least wondering—about the creativity possessed by the *subjects* of my future theories.

LAST YEARS AT COWLES

My remaining time at Cowles—from 1963 to the fall of 1965— began tragically with the assassination of President Kennedy. Those of us at the Cowles Foundation went to the adjacent parking lot where we listened as the wrenching news unfolded on a car radio. Jim Tobin, Bill Brainard, T. N. Srinivasan, and one or two others were there, waiting for more information on Kennedy's condition. We were all shaken and said very few words. None of us would ever forget the final words of Walter Cronkite, CBS's news anchor: "The president was pronounced dead at 2 pm." I think we all felt that we had lost a light offering the country a new direction. Frost's line came to mind: "So dawn goes down today. / Nothing gold can stay."

Certainly, Kennedy's death was a blow to Jim and the others at Cowles who had been working or consulting in the government. They did not appear to be close to the Lyndon Johnson administration in the 1960s—nor to the Carter administration in the 1970s. Okun later moved to Washington, joining the Brookings Institution, and Brainard took on a role of running the semiannual Brookings meetings at which the Brookings Papers on Economic Activity were presented. Jim was a regular at those meetings, but Cowles no longer had a presence inside the federal government.

Yet the loss of its connection to the government—thus a significant loss of excitement and stimulus—was not the worst problem for economics at Yale. After my year's absence at MIT, I began to see economics at Yale in a different way. Debreu, a big figure in mathematical economics, had left. While some significant ideas were coming out of those working on underdevelopment at the Economic Growth Center—a slew of papers and a book, *The Theory of Integration*,[18] by Bela Balassa (who was forced to flee communist Hungary) and a book, *Development of the Labor Surplus Economy*,[19] by Gustav Ranis, an émigré from Nazi Germany (both friends of mine)—it was becoming clear by the mid-1960s that less theoretical work was coming out of the Cowles Foundation. (David Cass extended the Ramsey model of optimal national saving, and Tjalling Koopmans saw some deep conceptual difficulties in Ramseyian models.)

In my last three semesters working at Cowles, I wrote another small book: *Golden Rules of Economic Growth*.[20] Almost every model in that book replaces some central force taken to be a given in the original model—such as the saving-income ratio in the Solow–Swan growth model—with a variable that is the optimum size of that force. My earlier paper, "The Golden Rule of Accumulation," did the same thing. To my mind, the most interesting example (and the most far-out) was the one on the optimum proportion of the homogeneous workforce assigned to do industrial research rather than production. It was found to be a fixed number—and easily remembered. (One day, seeing Paul Samuelson in an elevator about to leave, I shouted, "Did you read my paper?" He shot back, "I saw the one-half," referring to one of the results.)

Nor did there appear to be a great deal of influential empirical research coming out of Cowles at this time either. Jim recruited Solow, von Weizäcker, Menahem Yaari, and me to a research unit—the Future of U.S. Economic Growth (FUSEG)—but its output was slim and the unit soon dissolved. The problem was that this group of ours had no idea what the source of the most advanced economies' growth was. This was not a very stimulating environment for any young economic theorist such as myself.

The big problem lay elsewhere. In the Economics Department as a whole, there was a considerable degree of the remarkable heterogeneity that had grown up in the 1950s. But at Cowles, an accepted theoretical foundation in thinking about the economy had developed, and any deviation from this body of thought was found ridiculous or irritating. Our main task was to shore up Keynes's theory or find further implications, not to create one or more new theories. My book on the public debt, which deviated from Jim's views in seeing debt, and thus the deficits that create it, as slowing growth, was never spoken of. The atmosphere at Cowles, then, did not invite, let alone encourage, new thinking.

I was not the only young colleague of Jim's who encountered his conformism. Years later, another young theorist at the Cowles Foundation, Pentti Kouri had a worse experience. In 1978–1979, Pentti, a new resident of New York after a few years at Cowles and a highflier working on financial matters with George Soros, dropped in to see me and Roman Frydman. The subject of Cowles came up, and Pentti became livid as he told us that his experience at Cowles had been destroying his "creativity." I never saw him so disturbed before or after. This narrowness in Jim extended to the classroom. A former student of mine once told me that some graduate students of economics at Yale were so outraged by the exclusion of the breakthrough developments in unemployment and inflation theory that they were contemplating a class-action suit against Yale.

It became clear, then, that Jim was pained when someone close to him took a different view. And he had a hard time dealing with it. As a result, we had a certain estrangement between us for the rest of his life. I was saddened by this, of course. There had been times before the estrangement when Jim was very generous to me—before I went my own way. He had picked me out for a private tutorial in macroeconomics in my second year of graduate work. There were also times after the estrangement when Jim was very kind. He told me he had "something to do" with my election to the National Academy of Science in 1982 (when I was only forty-nine). To my amazement, he was reported to have said at a session on economics textbooks at the annual meeting of the American Economic Association around 1986 that my textbook, *Political Economy*, was the best introductory text since the textbook of the great Irving Fisher.[21] At an event at Yale in 2000, which was to be our last together, he said to my wife, "I was wrong about Ned."

In early 1965, as I approached the last academic year of my contract with Yale, another problem arose. Several assistant professors over the past years had been promoted to a position of tenure—and with surprisingly few publications in a major journal, if any. So, I had come to believe that I, too, would be given tenure. I had written many articles and a book. When still in my fifth year, however, I was notified by the Economics Department that I would not be put up for tenure. My colleague Bela Balassa, for whatever reason, also left Yale.

The ugly part was that Bela and I had been publishing at a good rate and gaining an international reputation—in sharp contrast to those who were awarded tenure. This was not tragic, because we were bound to find good positions elsewhere, but the best possible openings were not plentiful. I was fortunate enough to land a full professorship at the University of Pennsylvania effective in autumn 1966. Bela went to Johns Hopkins, but died of cancer several years later.

It is true that President Griswold had notified the department head that he did not want to create more tenure positions. But it is also true that the senior department members had been eager to get tenure for the people they wanted for their own reasons. I was disgusted with these faculty members for being so self-interested and indifferent to the promise of their stellar young scholars. I learned from Gus Ranis that, when my tenure and Griswold's warning came up, Willie Fellner said, "Let's fight it," but no one joined him. The department (as well as Cowles), I learned, was largely under Tobin's control on key decisions. I even heard that Jim kept a small bell at his side to use if necessary to end discussions.

But, most important, over the year 1965, I became aware that in my time at the Cowles Foundation, I had not set out to do what got me into the economics profession to begin with. I had gone to graduate school and then on to a research center to try to connect the macroeconomics in the textbooks—namely, the theory created by Keynes—to the microeconomics in the textbooks—namely, the neoclassical theory rising from Carl Menger, Léon Walras, and Alfred Marshall to Frank Ramsey, Arthur Pigou, and Debreu.

Winding up my time at Yale, I left New Haven in January for a half-year in London and Cambridge, heading back to the United States in late summer for my new post at the University of Pennsylvania. There would be no going on with routine model building—with applied research. I felt liberated and ready to create new theories.

2

A NEW DIRECTION

Uncertainty and Expectations

Reaching London in early January 1966, with seven months at the London School of Economics (LSE) and Cambridge ahead of me and the prospect of my new position at the Wharton School of the University of Pennsylvania, I felt the time had come to try to address elements lacking in the standard macroeconomic theory of that time—certainly not to throw that theory away. The omission most on my mind was present in standard microeconomics as well as macroeconomics.

I worked hard in Room Q of the LSE library—generally the first to arrive and the last to leave—but it was hard to shut out the opportunities that city held. In the British theater of the 1960s, I was thrilled to take in the plays of Harold Pinter. I had caught in New York his early work *A Slight Ache*, in which Edward's understanding of what he reads does not reflect the modern world. I was lucky to see in London the opening run of *The Homecoming*, which also presented people bewildered over how little they knew. Any academic had to be struck when, after Lenny's appeal to Teddy, a British philosophy professor in America, for an answer to his question on how to live, the philosopher replies, "It's not my field." (The Beatles forecasted an improvement with "Here Comes the Sun" in 1969.)

One couldn't help but feel the rejections of the old and see that the search for a new direction was brewing. Among some economists, there was a feeling that parts of economic theory were not fully in touch with life in the economies of modern nations. Reminiscing over some of our early work over lunch a few years ago, Duncan Foley, a highly respected economist at the New School and the Santa Fe Institute, exclaimed that the 1960s were by far the most creative decade in economic theory since the 1930s. It was in 1966 that new steps in macroeconomic theory began. I was excited to be "present at the creation" and at the forefront of this work.

The ground for fundamental change had been broken by Frank Knight in his book *Risk, Uncertainty and Profit*.[1] There he had introduced the presence of "uncertainty"—also known as "Knightian uncertainty"—particularly among investors (and, one could add, savers too) in a market economy.[2] As a consequence, the volume of investment and the market value placed on the current capital stock, too, are not wholly determined— not even largely determined in a forward-looking economy— by the elements of neoclassical theory: saving, the real interest rate, wage rate, wealth, and the capital stock. High uncertainty (or ambiguity) and the resulting hunches and guesswork exert a powerful and variable force acting on all prices and quantities in the economy.

This was a profound departure from the neoclassical models built by Knut Wicksell, Irving Fisher, Joseph Schumpeter, Arthur Pigou, and Frank Ramsey early in the twentieth century—and, for that matter, from the stochastic models of portfolio selection introduced by Harry Markowitz in 1952 and by my 1962 paper "The Accumulation of Risky Capital."[3] Obviously, a high level of Knightian uncertainty—not risk, which has outcomes, each

occuring with known probabilities, but genuine uncertainty—
opened the door to misdirected investment and led to far too
little or far too much investment demand at many firms and
far too little or far too much lending by banks. Yet Knight's
advance, taken alone, did not show or imply that this uncertainty
could sometimes be a force driving the wide swings of employment in the modern economies of the past two centuries:
in the United States, the Long Depression of 1873–1879, the
Depression of 1882–1893, the 1920s Boom, the Great Depression
of 1929–1941, and the 2008 Great Financial Crisis. There was a
missing link.

John Maynard Keynes and Friedrich Hayek were the first
to apply this insight to the troubled economies in the United
States, Britain, and continental Europe in the 1930s. Their
sharp disagreements set off unprecedented fireworks in the
learned journals. Hayek argued in his *Prices and Production* that
the Depression was in fact a result of overinvestment.[4] When
much investment proved to be unprofitable so that the capital stock got "ahead of itself," investment was cut back below
its normal, equilibrium amount until the excess capital was
worked off—died of aging or use. Although it was clear that
rises and falls in investment could generate some vibration—
some short-term fluctuation—in aggregate investment activity and thus employment, was this sufficient to explain the
big swings in economic activity in the 1920s, the 1930s, and
the 2000s?

Keynes in his *General Theory of Employment, Interest and
Money* offered a *monetary* explanation of the Depression.[5] He
considers an economy in which people draw on the stock of
money to buy the goods that people are employed to produce:
If people have decided to buy less for some time, then the initial

impact of the resulting rise in the demand for money and corresponding drop in the demand for goods (i.e., a drop of "aggregate demand") is to force widespread cutbacks in production and
employment.[6] A recovery would begin, however, if the money
wage were to fall a suitable amount, driving down prices and, in
that way, raising the real value of the money supply, thus restor-
ing aggregate demand and hence regaining the equilibrium level
of output and employment.

Yet, as Keynes observed, a drop of investment demand, such
as results from a loss of "animal spirits" in Keynes's imagery, does
not in practice trigger a fall of money wage rates sufficient to pull
employment back to some normal level, let alone to forestall the
fall of output and employment that would otherwise occur. As
labor economists came to say, there is considerable "stickiness" in
wage rates. This was Keynes's theory of depressions. (*If* there were
no such stickiness, such that an immediate drop of the money
wage would occur, that would cause other problems. So, Keynes
was content with his theory.) It was not widely understood,
however, until John Hicks represented it in something like a
diagram of supply and demand—the investment and savings–
liquidity and money (IS-LM) diagram—in his 1937 paper "Mr.
Keynes and the 'Classics.'"[7]

Curiously, this theory had been lifted to the status of holy
scripture. Keynes, in trying to keep things as simple as possible,
had said wage rates were "sticky"—meaning that the average
wage could move only slowly—and let it go at that. He had proclaimed the general theory of employment without offering a
theory of wage-setting by firms. I decided I should think about
the determination of wage rates in the economy. It would be my
first effort toward a macroeconomics founded on a microeconomic base.

INTRODUCING EXPECTATIONS INTO
UNEMPLOYMENT THEORY

All this was on my mind as I settled into work mode in London. I worked every day at LSE, where the Economics Department was still basking in its days of glory under the leadership of Lionel Robbins who in 1931 recruited Hayek, a new voice in economics, to be a counterweight to the rising influence of Keynes in Cambridge. (I met Robbins, an impressive figure, and observed him engage with Fritz Machlup in a brilliant conversation spanning British politics to Wagner's Ring Cycle when dropping them off at Princeton after the close of the Amherst's Merrill Center.)

LSE's economics department in the 1960s could boast among its leading figures Richard Layard, Harry Johnson, Richard Lipsey, and, above all, A. W. Phillips, the economic statistician who had only recently caused a sensation with his "Phillips Curve."[8] I seldom saw anyone while I worked in Room Q off the library, but I had coffee with faculty members, such as Harry Johnson and Max Steuer—both became close friends of mine—and I could talk a little with them about what I was working on. It was great fun talking with the other visiting Americans, including Dick Caves and Ron Jones, on things noneconomic from John Huston's *Maltese Falcon* to Laurence Olivier's *Hamlet* playing in London.

In Room Q, I had a seminal thought. If firms are generally setting wages annually, say, not every season or month, then the typical firm hit by the drop of investment demand will *not* want to trim very much the usual raise to employees, let alone to decrease wages, if its expectations are that the other firms— those with which it competes and those in its city or town—are not going to be trimming the wages they pay. So, expectations of the rate at which wages are changing in the economy as a whole are of key importance for the actual rate of change of wage rates. If these expectations adjust only slowly, wage rates will tend to adjust slowly, too. As a result, the adjustment of money wages to a slump in aggregate demand will generally be slow; if the slump is mild, there may be no adjustment at all. In my view, this insight provided the missing link in Keynes's theory of depression that assertions of "wage stickiness"—and, similarly, statistical estimates of a Phillips curve—did not. A general theory of employment requires a theory of wage behavior since wages have effects on employment. (In contrast, Keynes *had* seen he needed a theory of consumption, hence his postulate of a "consumption function.")

The formulation of wage behavior that I had conceived was radically different from Phillips's formulation. The former is microeconomic in that it derives from a conception of the decision-making of individual firms, whereas the Phillips curve is *not* micro-based: It is essentially a statistical estimate of a mechanistic hypothesis—thus, my formulation came to be termed "micro-macro." Furthermore, my formulation derives from the recognition that in any *modern* economy, each wage setter must make their decisions with little or no knowledge of what the other wage setters are deciding: They are all operating under a distinctive kind of (Knightian) uncertainty.

Exploring further the implications of such expectations, I managed while at LSE to explore and develop a model of a theoretical economy built around price expectations and behavior of that nature—a model with which to analyze fiscal stimulus. The model postulates that the rate of inflation depends on the rate of unemployment and the *expected* rate of inflation. (That expectation, I sensed, would be more convenient to work with than the expected change of money wages.) The other three ingredients of the model are (1) a "mechanism by which the expected inflation rate adjusts to the actual inflation rate," (2) the "utility" derived from the time path of consumption, and (3) the relationship between the current "rate of utility" and the "utilization" of production capacity.

Among this model's predictions are the following: A tight fiscal policy causing underutilization of the labor force will drive the inflation rate *below* the currently expected inflation rate; and a loose policy causing overutilization of the labor force leads to inflation *above* the expected rate. This model features what I dubbed the "warranted," or "equilibrium," rate of unemployment, which was later called the "natural" rate.

My main aim, however, was normative. Optimally, macro policy is more than just managing fluctuations in output and employment. It is also managing inflation. So, the task was to determine the properties of the optimal path of the economy in terms of employment, or capacity utilization, *and* what, given that path, would be the accompanying path of the rate of inflation, given the initially expected rate of inflation. In short, I needed to determine what would be the rule for maximizing "utility." From this point of view, advocates of a high-pressure policy of overutilization of labor—of pulling unemployment below its warranted level—are being short-termist: In favoring high utilization today at the cost of high inflation in the future equilibrium, they reveal high "time preference."[9] (This may remind the reader of the governments accused in the previous decade of austerity. Of course, the unplanned deficits following the COVID-19 outbreaks were inevitable and the planned deficits were justifiable.)

With this crude model and the analysis of it, I had broken away from both the neoclassical theory of perfect decision-making—based on the postulate's perfect information and complete knowledge—and another model focused on wage behavior was on the way. Dynamical models of this sort are a methodological step forward from the statistical approach—that is, the reliance on a relationship between one variable of interest and another as long as it is plausible and meets the condition for statistical significance. Of course, it would have been naïve to base any economic policy-making on theoretical explorations of such a highly abstract model.

After leaving London on the first of May and taking a vacation on the Continent centered around Budapest, Vienna, and the Salzburg music festival, I began my visit to Cambridge.

At Cambridge and Oxford, some important figures from the revolutionary 1930s remained: at Oxford, I met John Hicks and Roy Harrod; and at Cambridge, I met James Meade and Joan Robinson, a prominent member of the legendary Cambridge Circus.

Professor Robinson was a formidable presence, and it was with some trepidation that I went to see her over tea one afternoon. Wasting no time on pleasantries, she launched into an exposition of her recent thought. I didn't understand her and asked a question, but I didn't understand her answer either. I tried again, but she gave up. "You could understand," she said, "if you wanted to."

Later in the spring, I gave a talk in Cambridge on my new work on expectations. Most of the stars were there—Frank Hahn, James Mirrlees, Partha Dasgupta, and James Meade. I felt the discussion that ensued after I had finished my presentation was going well enough, particularly considering that not one of them was in macroeconomics. But Meade complained that I had given him a headache! I consoled myself that a new theory is not quickly grasped, and I had to do better in my expositions.

Over the three months in Cambridge, I worked on my second model built around expectations. It was a model of an economy using money, thus having money prices and money wages, and expectations of the expected rate of change of nominal wages—the "money wage," as Keynes called it. This model, after some further work in the autumn, was presented in a working paper and subsequently a conference paper discussed later.

This visit, besides providing a home for my research at an important point in my development, was also the source of long friendships with Partha Dasgupta and the late Jim Mirrlees. Even the fierce Frank Hahn commented the last time we met that I was "going up, up, up." I appreciated the brilliance of the Cambridge economists and their openness to others' ideas.

With my arrival at Penn in August 1967, I had a sense of liberation that lasted throughout my years there; my theoretical work and historic conference I held there were, for many decades, the most exciting part in my professional life.

It was also a joy to be in Philadelphia after so many years in New Haven. My home was the top-floor apartment on Rittenhouse Square, not far from the School of Music, with some sunshine all day long. From there it was a long walk past the Philadelphia Museum of Art to the University of Pennsylvania and the Wharton School where the Economics Department was located, physically and administratively; I often took that walk after a busy day. It was an easy walk to the art galleries and not far from the old Temple of Music. There I heard Jon Vickers and the unequalled Birgit Nilsson perform in *Tristan und Isolde*. In a cavernous hall a mile away, I heard an unforgettable performance by the breathtaking Franco Corelli and Nilsson in *Turandot*. For several days, I couldn't get Corelli's sound out of my head. (Luciano Pavarotti declared in one of his last televised interviews that Corelli was the "greatest dramatic tenor who has ever lived.")

Yet, I wasn't confined to Philadelphia. Although my break from standard macro was only slowly noticed, I had evidently become established as an expert in macroeconomics. In November, I received a phone call from Edwin Kuh, whom I had gotten to know at MIT, inviting me to be part of a small group of economists. This group, to which he also belonged, would convene from time to time in Boston and make reports on various subjects for Robert Kennedy, who was preparing to seek the presidential nomination by the Democratic Party. Also in the group was Jim Tobin representing Yale, Marty Feldstein from Harvard, Art Okun from Brookings, and one or two others. Jim spoke about fiscal and monetary policy, and I recall giving a presentation on wages and unemployment. This was the first time I came in direct contact with an influential government figure.

I got to know Kennedy a tiny bit. I was a cigar smoker in those years, and he would occasionally ask me for one. When he was killed in June, the whole country was in shock, and I felt a personal loss, wondering what might have been. Going to the railway tracks, I watched the train bearing his casket pass by on its way from Washington, DC, to New York. Seeing the funeral at St. Patrick's Cathedral on television, I was moved when Andy Williams, with that beautiful voice of his, rose from his seat in the congregation to sing a cappella the "Battle Hymn of the Republic."

Almost exactly a year later I received a phone call from Arnold Harberger inviting me to be a part of a task force to advise President-elect Richard Nixon on how best to deal with the rising inflation that was becoming a subject of much discussion. Al had been helpful with my book on public debt, so I didn't want to reject the invitation out of hand. I told Al that I was a Democrat, not a Republican like Nixon, but Al said that didn't matter. So, I joined the task force, participating in its long meeting over a weekend in New York. I was irked that our report, written by Al, did not reflect the view I had expressed at our meeting.

Some weeks later, a banquet was held for the twenty task forces at the Hotel Pierre to express Nixon's appreciation for their work. In the receiving line, Nixon stretched out his hand and asked me what task force I was on. When I said I was on the one on inflation, Nixon exclaimed, "I want to reduce the inflation without causing more unemployment, but Arthur Burns said that's impossible." I felt this packed room with its long line behind me was not the place to try to convey my thinking on the subject.

As it turned out, neither Nixon nor I could know that in the late 1970s Paul Volcker, on becoming head of the Fed, would conquer the "dragon of inflation" with collateral damage more short-lived than had been feared. Yet for months, there was anxiety that Volcker's tight money might bring a shocking increase of unemployment when—or even before—the inflation rate was subdued. In a dinner of the Brookings Panel on Economic Opportunity with Chairman Volcker at the height of the anxiety, I got up to say that what was needed was to calm the *expectations* of high inflation. Paul seemed slightly amused (he and I became good friends in his last two decades).

Important though such exchanges with government figures may be, I had decided to make my career in universities to do research, not in the public sector. So I lost no time at Penn in getting back to the development of a new kind of macroeconomic theory: one in which the actors in their decision-making have neither full information about what is happening elsewhere nor full knowledge of how the economy works. I resumed my work, begun over the summer at Cambridge, on a theoretical model in which the typical firm is engaged in setting its own money wages on the basis of its information on nominal wages elsewhere and its expectation of the rate of change of nominal wages at other firms. Hence, this model of the economy is generally not on an equilibrium path in the sense of a path along which outcomes bear out expectations—but is instead generally found working its way under conditions of expectations not borne out, that is, *disequilibrium.*

Out of this work, I developed a theoretical model of a monetary economy that differs from both Keynes's postulate (in his *General Theory*) of a money wage level that is a constant for all practical purposes and Phillips's postulate of a money wage that will be rising or falling mechanically according to the volume of unemployment—that is, according to where the economy lies on the Phillips curve. Of course, the model can be described by a system of equations, one of which describes the determinants of the rate of wage change. It can also be described by diagrams—just as Hicks used a diagram to describe Keynes's theory and Phillips used a diagram to illustrate his curve. But the system of equations describing my theory of money wages, employment, and inflation in both equilibrium and disequilibrium are derived from a theory—from *microeconomic* foundations. Unfortunately, the rate-of-wage-change equation, in containing the Phillips curve relationship among other relationships, came to be called the "augmented Phillips Curve," although the Phillips relationship was not any more important than the other relationships and Phillips's curve did not have any theoretical foundation. His hypothesis may have received some statistical support, but the model I built has an explicit theoretical basis.

I would make three comments about the model. First, regarding the setting in which labor-market decisions are made, workers and firms are not continuously informed of the actions of one another. They meet randomly at a frequency depending on the number of workers unemployed, hence searching for a job, and the number of job vacancies. The hiring rate in the economy—the quit rate too—depends on the current unemployment rate and current vacancy rate.

Second, regarding the individual firm, its quit rate will depend negatively on its wage relative to the average of other firms; and its hiring rate will depend positively on the same relative wage. Accordingly, a firm's hiring will depend positively on its quit rate, the relative size of its wage as well as on the rate of unemployment, and negatively on the aggregate vacancy rate. A firm, given its vacancies, will try to establish a wage relative to its expectations of wages elsewhere that depend positively on their own vacancies as well as on the aggregate vacancy rate, and negatively on the rate of unemployment. In this economy, neither price nor quantity is determined by "supply and demand." The market is characterized by the presence of both unemployed workers and job vacancies owing to insufficient, or "imperfect," information.

Third, the equation system that constitutes the model can be boiled down to just two equations: one giving the rate of change of the average money wage and the other giving the rate of change of employment. We can then analyze the motion of the two variables using standard methods.

This model-building and analyzing led—in my view, at any rate—to *two* principal propositions. One has to do with understanding unemployment and the other with inflation.

First, if an economy with unemployment initially at its normal level and inflation running at the expected rate suffers a drop of demand, a gradual loss of employment will occur because markets will not reduce wages, and hence prices, fast enough to avert any fall of output, and hence employment—thus not averting a rise of unemployment. (Again, Keynes simply postulated that the "money wage" is "sticky" and offered no way to think about—let alone predict in any quantitative way—the magnitude of the rate of the slowdown of wages.) Such a theoretical construct, if made the basis for econometric estimation, would tend to provide a better basis for predictions and explanations than an econometric estimation of a Phillips curve. At the very least, such an econometric estimation had better incorporate estimated expectations of rates of price and wage inflation.

Second, the model, in hypothesizing that the unemployment rate (or its rate of change) is related to the rate of wage inflation *net* of the expected rate of wage inflation (and, in principle, the rate of price inflation possibly net of the expected rate of price inflation), implies that an equal rise (or fall) of the expected and actual rates of inflation will be "neutral" with regard to unemployment. This led to the concept of an "inflation-corrected Phillips Curve." (Such neutrality, which goes back to Abba Lerner and William Fellner and which Milton Friedman popularized, became a subject of wide discussion for several years.)

I had a feeling that this development of economic theory would have an enduring effect on the way economists think about wage inflation, hence inflation of prices and swings in employment; and whatever happened to my paper illustrating the importance of imperfect information, the body of macroeconomics would not be the same. Decades later, this contribution has come to seem lasting. Peter Howitt, some forty years later in a 2007 *Scandinavia Journal of Economics* article wrote:

> Edmund Phelps helped change the way we think about macroeconomic theory and policy, by introducing imperfect information and costly communication into the theory, and deriving their implications for the dynamics of inflation and unemployment.

Phelps treated macroeconomics as a social science, whose subject matter is not just the choices people make but how people interact in groups. His pioneering efforts in developing a formal theory of the coordination mechanisms governing interactions led the way to a new kind of macroeconomics, one that was based on the interplay between the actions and expectations of individual actors, instead of being based on postulated relationships between macro aggregates.[10]

I was pleased by his observation that this new work of mine revolved around individuals—people with their own expectations and beliefs.

My first draft of a paper with a historical introduction and an exposition of the theory, "A Theory of Money Wage Dynamics and Its Implications for the Phillips Curve," appeared in February 1968 in the Pennsylvania Discussion Paper Series. It must have been around that time that Harry Johnson, Chicago-LSE professor and editor of both the *Journal of Political Economy (JPE)* and *Economica*, invited me to give a paper on my subject of the dynamics of wages and unemployment at the fifth Conference of University Professors on macroeconomic theory and trade theory in Montauk, Long Island, in late spring. A great many of the glitterati were there: Milton Friedman, Lord Robbins, Jim Tobin, Henry Wallich, and Martin J. Bailey. My discussant was Axel Leijonhufvud, fresh from writing *The Economics of Keynes and Keynesian Economics*, the best book at that time on Keynes's theory.[11] It couldn't be said that the participants rushed to embrace the new theory I was propounding, but they were not hostile to it either; they needed some time to digest it. The papers, including my "Money-Wage Dynamics and Labor-Market Equilibrium," were quickly collected and published by the *JPE* in their August 1968 edition.[12]

With this landmark in my thinking at that time, I was happy not only to have introduced a better structure into the foundation of Keynesian theory—at one of its crucial points—but also to have been engaged with others in the ongoing development of what was perhaps the most discussed area of economic theory at that time. I felt I was at the frontier of economic theory. This was radical stuff. It was very rewarding to me but, as I soon realized, I had miles to go.

It may have been sensed, even recognized, by a few economists that an important change in the way to think about labor markets and perhaps product markets, too, had emerged in 1967 and early 1968; it looked to me that more discussion and persuasion was needed. I was also excited to see evidence that similar thinking was beginning to take place in locales outside the Ivy League and Chicago—from Rochester to Northwestern to Los Angeles. Seeing some of this new work, I began to explore the idea of an extraordinary conference built around the newfound importance of expectations and beliefs in any economy rife with imperfect information and knowledge. With a subsidy from the National Science Foundation, I was able over several months to recruit a gathering of the largely young economists breaking away from the dogma of the older generation.

The big conference took place at Penn in late January 1969. Day 1, on wage dynamics and employment, began with the paper by Armen Alchian on the costs of gathering more information for better decisions. A paper by Charles Holt pointed to sociological and institutional factors giving rise to sticky wage rates. I slotted my "Money-Wage Dynamics" paper next because of seniority and the fact that the first version had been published just five months earlier. In the next paper, Dale Mortensen proposed to go deeper than my paper on wage dynamics. I was not unhappy to see the development of a more detailed model than the one I had set out. Last, in a different spirit, Robert Lucas and Leonard Rapping offered a fundamentally neoclassical model of a changing labor market in which prices and wage rates clear the market though some people are waiting for better offers—a model excluding the sort of imperfect information that cause wage rates to fail to clear the market.

Day 2 of the conference started with the paper Sidney Winter and I wrote, Optimal Price Policy under Atomistic Competition.[13] Just as the firm's stock of employees is part of its capital in my "Money-Wage Dynamics" paper, in my paper with Sid, the firm's stock of customers is a kind of capital—and, for simplicity, a firm's customers are the only capital it wants or needs. So, the price that the capital market would put on a firm would reflect the "shadow price" of the firm's stock of customers. The result is some remarkable parallels between the Phelps–Winter model and my model of wages and employment. In this economy, there is no Walrasian auctioneer able to set firms' prices at what the market will bear. A firm has to set its price (just as it had to set its wage in "Money-Wage Dynamics"), while using only highly imperfect information about the prices being set by the other firms. So, if it sees a drop in demand for its output—I thought always of restaurants—it does not know whether other firms have, on average, seen a similar drop. Hence, the price level moves sluggishly (i.e., is sticky), so reduced demand would go on depressing output and possibly employment, too. In an open-economy version developed and tested against data, it is found that a depreciation of a country's currency, in serving to protect firms from competitors from abroad, induces them to boost their markups, thus decreasing the country's output and employment. Lastly, the paper by Donald Gordon and Allan Hynes presented a theory to explain "disequilibrium dynamics," the presence of which had been described by theorists, such as Samuelson, but the origins of which had not.[14]

The advances in macroeconomic theory made at this conference spread like wildfire with the appearance in 1970 of the conference volume, *Microeconomic Foundations of Employment and
Inflation Theory*, published by W. W. Norton—my publisher for
two decades. Jeffrey Sachs at a Columbia event in 2006 recalled
the excitement he and other economics students felt on the
arrival of the book in the Harvard Square bookstore. Very few
times would I feel that much satisfaction again. I would be the
last to deny the importance of the experience of work on the
whole and, of course, the invaluable experience of rewarding
work. I have had such experience over my entire working life.
But there is also a thrill that comes from making a difference
and, in particular, from changing—in one respect or another—
the thinking of a large number of the people in one's industry or
profession.

In my view, what I did was to spearhead a movement to abandon the neoclassical view of the firm as a wage-taker as well as
a price-taker, so the firm has only to decide its production and
employment levels, given the wages and prices. This movement
intended also to abandon Keynes's halfway house of firms that
may very well not lower their wage levels appreciably, or at all,
in a slump. Among the theories that came out in place of both
the neoclassical model and Keynes's model was an embryonic
"micro-macro theory"—a very informal theory—of how financial gambles, technological developments, and structural forces
drive the economy up or down (whether or not forward). What
I had done was beginning to be done by others—and, no doubt,
sometimes done better. (It should be noted that the existence
and possible importance of expectations had been brought up
in Keynes's 1937 *General Theory* with his discussion of "average
opinion" in the stock market and in Hayek's 1948 *Individualism and Economic Order* with his discussion of the "utilization of

knowledge which is not given to anyone in its totality"—so "one person will base his plans . . . on the expectation that other people will act in a particular way."[15] The role that inflation expectations played was studied in Philip Cagan's 1956 statistical study.[16] I was apparently the first to make expectations a theoretical basis for Keynes's assumption, or tenet, that wages generally exhibit "stickiness.")

Furthermore, in my view, these papers were at the frontier in bringing to economists some sense of a dimension of economic life not appearing in neoclassical economics and Keynesian economics, too. For the many who have to make decisions— professional decision makers, of course, but also small business owners and working families—the economy described in most of the papers in the conference volume can be a scary place. Of course, such an economy can be exciting and rewarding, too.

In the last section of my introduction to *Microeconomic Foundations*, I observed that "a common thread runs through all these (un-classical) models. The actors in each of the models have to cope ignorant of the future or even much of the present. Isolated and apprehensive, these Pinteresque figures construct expectations about the economy—over space and time—and try to maximize relative to that imagined world."[17] Thus, this work marks the beginning of a bridge to a broader sense of business life and human experience. It seemed to me that, in a way, our 1969 conference—an early study of people in the economy trying to understand what to do—was a fitting end to the 1960s, Pinter's decade.

My first years at Penn were not all taken up with my work on microfoundations for a new macroeconomics. I was surrounded by colleagues at Penn with whom I wrote (and published) several papers. With Karl Shell, I wrote "Public Debt, Taxation and Capital Intensiveness"; with Edwin Burmeister, I wrote "Money, Public Debt, Inflation and Real Interest"; and with Robert Pollak, I published "On Second-Best National Saving and Game-Equilibrium Growth."[18] I also put out my own "Population Increase."[19] Late one afternoon on a walk home from my office at Wharton, I thought about the five papers I had written in the space of a year or so and wondered whether I would ever have ideas at such a rate. (As it turned out, I produced a spate of papers until the early 1980s when I turned to writing books.)

Sometime in spring 1969, I got a mysterious message from Amartya Sen, who, though still at Oxford, was working for some months at the United Nations in New York, inviting me to join him for lunch in the city. We talked about many things, including some draft pages of a new book of his on welfare economics, *Collective Choice and Social Welfare*. I don't know whether he knew, but I told him that I had received a grant from the Brookings Institution to work for the next academic year in Stanford at the Center for Advanced Study in the Behavioral Sciences (CASBS). He told me that the Harvard philosopher John Rawls would also be there. I had not read much on economic welfare since college, although in graduate school, I had read some work by Jeremy Bentham and a standard text, *Theoretical Welfare Economics*, by J. de V. Graaff. Nonetheless, I was excited.

On United Flight 5 from Philadelphia to San Francisco in mid-August, headed to CASBS, I worked to complete my introduction to *Microeconomic Foundations*—delighted with its advance in theory. (It was on that flight that the image of "Pinteresque figures" acting in the economy came to mind.) I was thrilled once again to be going out west for a long stay, but this time, with nearly a decade's work in macroeconomics behind me, I had the feeling that I might be embarking on a new course.

3

UNEMPLOYMENT,
WORK'S REWARDS, AND
JOB DISCRIMINATION

I settled into the Center for Advanced Study in the Behavioral Sciences (CASBS) overlooking Stanford University as
soon as I found a place to live (a house in Mountain View)
and bought a car (a Jaguar). Among the Center's fellows that
year were some prominent figures. As expected, John Rawls (or
Jack) was writing *A Theory of Justice*. Richard Pipes and Samuel
Huntington were also there working on research, and I became
friends with them and many others, especially Jack for the rest
of his life. I also had warm friendships with the philosophers
Amélie Rorty and her then-husband Richard Rorty (on his way
to new ideas in philosophy and later the book *Achieving Our
Country*), Donald Davidson, Richard Brandt, and the psycholo-
gists Tracy and Howard Kendler.

Everyone came there to progress with their project, of
course, yet our year together in the Stanford Hills of the San
Francisco Peninsula was an idyll we would not forget. Some of
us played volleyball almost every day in the broiling sun. ("You
guys must be crazy," a physician said to one of us. I was never
in such good shape, though. A young woman in the office
said to Jack after I misplayed a ball, "Ned's beautiful, but he
can't play volleyball.") Together we coped with the troubling

developments in San Francisco, on the Stanford Campus, and right in the Center.

It would be difficult to exaggerate the outbreaks of protests that arose in the late 1960s and the 1970s in the United States—notably, the Watts riots in Los Angeles in 1965, the Long Hot Summer of 1967 in New York, the Columbia University protests of 1968, and the Third World Liberation strikes of 1968 at the University of California at Berkley and San Francisco State College. I recall taking a walk one afternoon in early spring from my office to the edge of the CASBS property and, looking down at the Stanford campus below, saw smoke curling up from Encina Hall, the central headquarters of the university. A band of protesters suspected of coming from San Francisco had set fire to the building.

A later attack came closer to home. The associate director, Preston Cutler, telephoned around four in the morning to report that arsonists had attacked two banks of studies, and my study was one of those that was hit. "You better get down here," he said. I have never forgotten the anxious drive to the Center. Maybe my manuscript, which I had no copies of, was ruined. Maybe Jack Rawls's manuscript was ruined. Maybe the Center would be closed for months. Fortunately, the Center was still functional, and our manuscripts survived. (My impression was that even the hardest hit were usable.)

With little doubt, this social unrest stirred interest in the subject of the working poor and the people suffering discrimination in the labor market among us at CASBS and other public-interest organizations. The Brookings Institution had already taken an interest. I met there in early 1968 with Joseph A. Pechman, who showed me data he had compiled on low-wage income in the bottom quintile of the distribution, and soon after,

I received a year-long grant from Brookings to prepare in 1968–69 a book on unemployment and low wages.

It was against this backdrop that I began working in my year at CASBS on unemployment, especially among low-wage earners—with the inattention to wage rates at the low end and the role of work—and on a desirable inflation policy in view of its impact on unemployment. The major output was the lengthy book, *Inflation Policy and Unemployment Theory: The Cost–Benefit Approach to Monetary Planning*, hereafter referred to as *Unemployment Theory*. (I was not sure about the title, especially the subtitle; so I asked Jack what he thought. He said, "It'll make the people mad you want to make mad." I was puzzled given that I wasn't out to get anyone. My interest was purely intellectual.)

The volume was mostly a study of unemployment from a number of perspectives—monetary as well as nonmonetary. Throughout, the book refers to a market economy that is predominantly private enterprise, such as the U.S. economy in those times. Most interesting is the nonmonetary part of this book, but it may be best first to touch on the monetary perspective.

The book begins with a survey of the contributions of economists to the understanding of the existence of unemployment and the fluctuations of an individual's unemployment and total unemployment. (The chapter tosses out the idea of what I dubbed "statistical discrimination," but more on this later.) The book then takes up the complicated relationships between the unemployment rate and inflation. On fluctuations, somewhat-neoclassical theories from Dennis Robertson and even Ludwig von Mises to Robert Lucas and Leonard Rapping, as well as Donald Gordon and Allan Hynes, appear in the text as do the "modern" theories of the labor market begun by myself and subsequently Dale Mortenson.

A significant contribution of the book lies in other aspects, though. *Unemployment Theory* marked the beginning of a series of my writings on the significance of the many facets, or dimensions, of work. Early in its discussion of employment, the book stresses that being employed brings "feelings of self-respect, esteem in the community, a sense of economic independence . . . and job satisfactions."[1] Later, noting "the social context of working, from comparing oneself to others," the book comments that "the creation of better job opportunities is likely to produce a gain in the dignity and self-respect of workers who catch those opportunities . . ."[2] (In subsequent years, the term "belonging" became widely used, though it does not appear to be used in *Unemployment Theory*.)[3] Writing just across the wall from me at CASBS was Rawls who comments in notes toward the end of *A Theory of Justice* that "perhaps the most important primary good is that of 'self-respect' . . . a person's sense of his own value," hence, as we might say, a person's sense that their life's work is worthwhile.[4]

The "job satisfactions" fleetingly referred to and barely touched on in *Unemployment Theory* earned more of my attention in the 1990s with *Rewarding Work* and came to lie at the core of my thinking in the following decades with *Mass Flourishing* in 2013 and *Dynamism* in 2020. In what might be called a good economy functioning in a good society, I argue, there are likely to be many "good jobs"—jobs that position people and open up opportunities to discover, explore, experiment, and even create. At this point in my thinking, however, creativity was not a concept I had arrived at yet.

Several inferences for macroeconomic policy might be drawn from these observations and themes. One is that any intertemporal model of optimal macroeconomic policy to be studied ought *not* to include only the standard variables of neoclassical economics—labor, capital, and land—as if unemployment does not exist. Also, the unemployment in the model must *not* be the unemployment that occurs as working people are constantly reallocating themselves for best results in the production process. In the model, then, unemployment is all bad. As I wrote, it "abstract[s] entirely from the function of unemployment as a provider of wage and job vacancy information."[5]

Although it was clear that other models of optimal macro policy toward inflation and unemployment were desirable, it was not clear how to proceed. Is the focus best placed on fiscal policy or on monetary policy? My 1967 paper, "Phillips Curves, Expectation of Inflation and Optimal Unemployment Over Time," presented a model of an economy needing no money, hence no monetary policy, to investigate optimal fiscal policy. I argued that if expectations of inflation are running high, considerations of long-term economic welfare require a bout of fiscal tightening to dampen those expectations, even though that will cause a surge of the unemployment above the "natural rate."[6]

Later in the book, I suppose that fiscal policy is tied up with other goals involving the public debt and national saving, so the instrument for the management of unemployment is monetary policy. Monetary policy is best based not simply on the goal of stabilizing the inflation rate around some notion of an optimal inflation rate target. Such a policy would let the unemployment rate take wide swings without the benefit of any stabilization. Yet a monetary policy of doing no more than trying to stabilize the unemployment rate around the level believed to be the best-maintainable level, such as that corresponding to estimates of the "natural rate of unemployment," would leave the economy vulnerable to wide swings of the inflation rate.

The book's discussion of monetary policy begins with an "illustrative model" of the "optimal inflation path" under rarefied conditions.[7] The model supposes that a "natural rate of unemployment" exists and that monetary policy supports recovery when unemployment is abnormally high. The book then determines optimal monetary policy in a simplified model of aggregate demand, inflation, and unemployment.

In the simplest case, the optimal policy gradually drives the expected inflation rate toward the level that gives maximum sustainable benefit.[8] As that rate is approached, of course, the unemployment rate approaches the natural rate. (In a more general case, the optimal unemployment rate under current expectations is such that the expected inflation rate is falling or rising at the appropriate pace.[9]) Equivalently, "the optimal policy may be viewed as increasing the current algebraic inflation rate up to the point where the 'marginal utility' . . . of that inflation rate equals the excess of the maximum sustainable utility rate over the current utility rate"—a formula much like that in Frank Ramsey's theory of optimal national saving.[10]

In the book, however, I recognize that in the modern world, any deterministic model of optimal monetary policy misses the enormous uncertainty about the future and, in some respects, the present too. As a consequence, policy makers may be inclined to throw away the rule book and follow their intuitions while markets are doing the same.

As I see it, although the book did not deliver a workable manual for the conduct of monetary policy, let alone a broader manual on the conduct of monetary and fiscal policy together, I did come closer to what an optimal monetary policy is about than Milton Friedman did when he advocated for a passive monetary policy and reliance on the market to do well. I also came closer to an optimal policy than Robert Lucas did when he envisioned leaving unemployment up to the supposedly rational expectations of the market. Moreover, it had become important to me that the book organized what was at that time the fullest discussion available of the importance of work and thus the depth of the nonpecuniary loss—however large or small the pecuniary loss—caused by unemployment for any long stretch of time.

In August 1970, with my year at CASBS behind me, I went back east to resume my duties teaching at the University of Pennsylvania while I decided to make my home in New York. I had made the difficult decision to decline a much-appreciated offer from Stanford. Yet, I also felt the need to live in New York—to catch up with the work of Leonard Bernstein at the New York Philharmonic, George Balanchine at the City Ballet, and James Levine at the Metropolitan Opera while they lasted. The living modernist figures in the performing arts were dwindling down.

In New York, my intellectual life began to broaden. One morning, when leaving my apartment to catch the elevator, I met the philosopher Thomas Nagel, who was living on the same floor. He knew I knew Rawls—Tom quoted Jack as having said I was "different from the other economists." On the train, I said I did not much like riding a crowded subway car to catch my train from Penn Station. Tom replied that he liked the crush of people in the subway car and the sweat of the crowd. (I suspect he was kidding about the sweat.) We interacted over the next three decades or more.[11]

In that year, although I wanted *most* to explore the implications of Rawlsian justice, I wanted *first* to explore further the idea of "statistical discrimination"—an idea introduced over a couple of pages in *Unemployment Theory*.[12] As I noted in that book, the theory fell naturally out of the non-Walrasian treatment of the labor market as operating imperfectly because of the scarcity of information about the existence and characteristics of workers and jobs.[13] (Incidentally, I always thought that "imperfect" was the right word and "asymmetric" was not. If I don't know, say, the demand I am facing and you don't know the demand I am facing, why is that called "asymmetric"?)

The following passages from the book conveyed the basic idea of statistical discrimination:

> Hiring biases may . . . be displayed in the choice between two [job applicants]. . . . The firm will likely latch on to such data as age, sex, height and weight, years of schooling, . . . previous jobs held—going on down a list that is dictated by the beliefs of the decision-maker about how performance in the job in question tends to be correlated with observations on such variables. The firm is engaging in [statistical estimation].
>
> . . . [Just as] a traveler might be said to be "discriminating" if, in the absence of local information, he makes it a rule to dine outside his hotel rather than inside it even though the restaurant selected will sometimes be inferior to the one at the hotel. . . . Similarly, a cost-minimizing firm may "discriminate" on the basis of a few data which it uses as proxies for some detailed description of the individuals that it does not believe to be economical or maybe even feasible to secure.[14]

In other words, skin color and gender are taken as proxies for relevant data not sampled. As I went on to say, social critics are asking whether we do not require in the labor market and elsewhere in society something more than blind justice and statistical fairness.

Sometime later, Edward Prescott and Karl Shell proposed I write an extension of this case. The resulting journal article was "The Statistical Theory of Racism and Sexism," in which I wrote, "The theory of discrimination originated by Gary Becker is based on the factor of racial taste. The pioneering work of Gunnar Myrdal also appears to center on racial antagonism."[15] In contrast, my paper, besides summarizing the noted discussion, also developed a mathematical model of this prevalent discrimination in hiring.

By 1971, with my book on monetary policy published and the offshoot, statistical discrimination completed, I was free again to undertake one or more new projects. Yet I was far from having set a new course. Certainly, I wanted to conceive something deep—something creative. But what that would be was unforeseeable. Meanwhile, I could explore Rawlsian justice and stand ready to address other topics gaining interest.

4

ALTRUISM AND RAWLSIAN
JUSTICE

While still in the midst of 1971, a piece of luck fore-shadowed new directions in my career and my work. One day on my usual train from Philadelphia back to Manhattan, I found myself sitting across from Kelvin Lancaster, an economics professor at Columbia who had become the chair of the Economics Department. It was clear that, after much aging and the Columbia riots in 1968, Columbia's department needed new senior members, and I felt the need to be fully in New York. I joined Columbia starting in the fall of 1971.

The 1970s were a time of a great deal of rethinking and soul-searching following the protests and violence of the 1960s. A great many new ideas were being hatched. I recall being invited by Arthur Bloomfield, a colleague at the University of Pennsylvania, to spend a weekend in the summer of 1971 at Sag Harbor in Long Island with Betty Friedan, author of the landmark *The Feminine Mystique*. A congenial member of congress present that weekend raised the matter of the lopsided income distribution in the country and started discussion of a big plan to redistribute incomes. In a chat with Betty in the parking lot later that day, I said she should be aware that such a scheme would require a huge amount of tax revenue, so its adoption would leave little room, if any, to finance other initiatives of great value to the country.

Amid all this ferment and my first year at Columbia coming up in September, I looked forward to getting into new work. My thoughts were shifting away from growth theory (first risky capital accumulation, then "golden rule," and so on), away from macroeconomic theory (public debt and fiscal policy, inflation and monetary policy, disequilibrium unemployment, and the role of imperfect information in expectations formation), and toward some other ideas that lie at the foundations of economic theory.

One such fundamental matter is the range of experience coming out of participation in economies—advanced ones, at any rate. In the usual view of a market economy, people work to earn money with which to meet the family's needs for nutrition, clothes, shelter, transportation, entertainment, vacation, and the like. Purporting to capture the essence of people's activity in a market economy, the standard textbook and model portrayed (and still portrays) participants as doing no more than weighing opportunities to earn, to spend, to save, and to invest in view of the prices and then making decisions—that is, the best possible decisions in the neoclassical theory or the less-than-best-possible in "behavioral economics" with its departures from "rational choice."

Yet these standard economic theories fail to account adequately for the gift-giving, donations, and philanthropic investing that many people occasionally do with the money coming from their income and capital gains after meeting their needs to spend and save, as well as with the time they have after meeting their needs to work. This phenomenon became increasingly widespread as more and more people had money and time to spare. In fact, people from mid-nineteenth century to the mid-twentieth century could increasingly afford to exercise altruism and display ethical standards to the extent they possessed these qualities—more so the greater the time and money they had for such acts. People made gifts to individuals and donations to philanthropic projects. People also exercised care in driving their cars and preparing food stuffs for sale. That is obvious now, but it was less so—even contested—at the time. (Another fundamental matter is society's redistribution, a formidable subject that was in the back of my mind, which I finally got to a year later.)

The lack of attention to the phenomena of altruism and ethical standards came to a halt early in the 1970s when a rush of economists, sociologists, and philosophers began to discuss the effects of altruism and morality in the economy, triggered evidently by the publication of the 1970 book *The Possibility of Altruism* by Princeton philosopher Thomas Nagel and the 1971 book *The Gift Relationship* by the London School of Economics (LSE) sociologist Richard Titmuss. It was surely a conversation or two with Tom that led me to think of organizing a conference on the subject and prompted me to ask Ken Arrow, whom I had learned was interested in Titmuss's book, to give the lead paper at the conference. Very quickly a brilliant group of theorists and philosophers were lined up, and Eleanor Sheldon at the Russell Sage Foundation agreed to provide logistical and financial support for a conference held in March 1972. The speakers, besides Ken, included Paul Samuelson, James Buchanan, William Vickrey, Roland McKean, William Baumol, Burton Weisbrod, and Bruce Bolnick. In addition to Tom, the discussants were Amartya Sen, Guido Calabresi, Sidney Morgenbesser, Edward McClennen, and Karl Shell. A stellar group.

It was good to see a number of philosophers and economists familiar with one another's work. There was no wall between philosophy and economics. Over the interwar period, too, there had been no wall between economists and philosophers at Cambridge, Oxford, Sciences Po, and other universities. There are, after all, some parallels between the questions asked in moral philosophy and the questions in normative "welfare economics." The conference furthered the importance of altruism. It was noted that, on some estimates, more than half the U.S. population depend for their security and material satisfactions not on the sale of their services but rather on their relationships to others. There was much interest in what economics can add to the understanding of altruistic behavior. "If a task of economists is to [explain] and evaluate allocation of resources," I commented, "then the analysis of altruistic resource use is a bridge to be crossed."[1]

One claim for altruism made in the introduction to the conference volume is that "the adherence to certain altruistic precepts and traditions by the participants in commercial markets makes a crucial contribution to the national income and thus, very likely, to Bentham–Bergson economic welfare."[2] One such precept is truthfulness. Arrow's paper argued that "truthfulness [by the seller] contributes in a very significant way to the efficiency of the economic system. The supplying of truthful information is an example of an externality. . . . [T]he two key features of the situation are uncertainty about the quality of the service and a difference between the degrees of knowledge possessed by buyer and seller."[3] A point I would make, which did not belong in the introduction nor in my paper, is that asking sellers in the marketplace to show altruism, or in Arrow's words "truthfulness"—a request that is not the same thing as asking start-ups with a new idea to share it immediately with the established firms in the industry—serves to remove or reduce the distrust that can obstruct the collaborations and agreements often needed to undertake new ventures—ventures into the unknown that are needed for sustained economic growth.

A wealth of papers and comments were shared at this sparkling conference—far too many to discuss here. I would add only that the deep paper by Peter Hammond presents a model in which "some charitable behavior could arise even in a world of total egoists, provided these egoists have appropriate expectations,"[4] and that my paper, building on the 1968 Phelps–Pollak model of game-equilibrium growth, exhibits a model in which the game-equilibrium path cannot be completely determined, yet "there may develop an 'ethic' that specifies some obligations that each generation is expected to meet. . . . [Thus] morals may make determinate the altruistic behavior of each generation."[5]

So, yes, altruism, including honesty toward others, reduces inefficiency in the allocation of resources and is likely to be hugely beneficial. The evident decline of such values over recent decades in the U.S. economy from Exxon to Purdue Pharma is a matter of considerable concern. Looking back at this conference, I am struck by the wooden character of the economies described or modeled there. I would have to say that they overlooked a significant dimension of working lives.

Those descriptions and models do not express the experience many, if not most, participants had in the economies widely engaged in exploring and creating as much as making money—most markedly in Britain from about 1820 to 1940 and in the United States from about 1850, but also at times in Germany and France. Many people did not just give money; they gave of themselves. For them, the economy was the setting in which many could express themselves—to make a difference, however small—and perhaps contribute to society. This may have been much more important than giving money. In this way, people could also carry out their personal development.

After that brilliant conference, economists had little follow-up interest, as far as I knew. The ensuing conference volume, *Altruism, Morality, and Economic Theory*, came out in 1975 with nearly all of the papers except for one by Paul Samuelson, but the volume received only one review, that by Peter Howitt in the *Canadian Journal of Economics* in 1976. However, the book's main theme—that altruistic values could be helpful—got the attention (somewhat accidentally) of economic and legal scholars at the University of Chicago.

George Stigler, who at that time was to Chicago's microeconomics what Milton Friedman was to its macroeconomics, had kindly invited me not once but twice to speak at the famous seminar on legal and economic issues held at the law school, and I had always begged off. But when he invited me yet again early in fall 1972, I felt I had to accept, especially since I had just finished the introduction to *Altruism* and the participants would not feel the material was old hat. Of course, I expected that the participants, all devout believers in laissez-faire, would not quickly agree with the arguments I would be making.

In Stigler's apartment, before bucking the fierce wind on the way to the law school, he told me he would be disagreeing with me. I was not prepared, however, for the wall of resistance that came at every point. After my initial presentation in which, among other examples, I suggested that if all people have the altruism to stop on a red light at street corners, the result is an expected gain for all—a collective good. Stigler began the discussion by saying that he might personally prefer to have no red lights. It was a way of saying that in some cases acting altruistically costs too much—for some people, at any rate. But it did not seem to me that this point, while applying in principle to a class of cases, renders altruism undesirable in general or in most cases. In the ensuing discussion, the criticism of altruism grew fierce, although I thought I was holding my own against the extreme positions being taken by Gary Becker, Richard Posner, and some other luminaries. With the seminar finally over, an old professor from the law school came up to me and said in his thick German accent, "Why did you agree at the end when you were doing so well?" He was referring, I think, to a point that—nearing exhaustion—I had conceded for the sake of argument. I felt bad that I had disappointed him. (Research suggests that he was Max Rheinstein, an eminent figure in jurisprudence.)

Although it was delightful to come up with the several ideas I had in the 1970s and to be able to write about them— ideas about monetary policy and unemployment, work's values, job discrimination, and altruism—it was my conversations with John Rawls and my reading of his great book, *A Theory of Justice*, that were coming more and more to occupy my thoughts.

In the years when his influence was growing on me, it was also growing on the country. In the words of a recent study, "John Rawls has had a profound influence on the American mind, altering how we understand justice, equity, liberty and constitutionalism."[6] I wrote several papers on Rawlsian matters over the course of the 1970s. His work led me to devote an entire chapter, "Ideas of Fairness," on views about income distribution—with his thesis at the center—in my textbook, *Political Economy*.

Rawls's great work begins by positing an abstract setting in which working people come together to form an economy for the realization of their goals. Before they start up, though, they will want to agree on the principle that will govern the distribution of the fruits of their efforts. A key point of Rawls's is that they will not agree to have equality. He understood that equal pay would come at a cost for everyone—including those with the least earning power, who badly need every dollar. (Rawls also understood that a minimum wage high enough to bring a decent living to those fortunate enough to keep their jobs would cost the less fortunate their jobs and thus their incomes, meager as they were.)

Rawls's thesis—in the setting to which he is referring—is that justice requires that the differences between the rewards of the more advantaged and the least advantaged are to be allowed up to the point at which any *larger* differences, or disparities, would *reduce* the reward of the least rewarded (i.e., the lowest earners). This distributive policy came to be called "maxi-min" since the lowest reward is to be lifted up to the maximum possible level. He reached this conclusion on the grounds that it would be agreed to by everyone if they did not know where they were going to find themselves in the wage distribution.

We could complain about focus on the very least advantaged group if, say, the next-to-least advantaged would have gained from a little more generosity to those super-able in the upper reaches. But those of us who have warmed to Rawls's "difference principle" have tended to view this complaint as nit-picking and have not been dissuaded from regarding it as the best principle of distributive justice we have. A theory of justice does not have to be perfect to be worth acting upon. It has only to be—for the time being—the best we have.

Rawls's thesis was a reaction against Jeremy Bentham's utilitarianism—a policy of redistributing in such a way as to maximize the "sum of utilities." In the utilitarian doctrine, not only is the utility of the person with the least utility not the thing to be maximized, it is not even clear whether the utilities to be summed up are the utilities of those working in the economy or of all those living in the nation—or even whether the utilities are those in the country or in the whole world.

I grew curious about what Rawls's policy, if instituted, would look like. Would marginal tax rates in the very-high-wage-income brackets be sky-high? Clearly the policy, whatever else it entails, means raising from the upper and middle levels of wage earners the maximum amount of tax revenue possible so as to enable the maximum amount of subsidies—negative taxes, so to speak—at the lower level of wage earners. In the Rawlsian spirit, the government has no higher use for that revenue. Needless to say, the least advantaged person among the employed is supposed to have a productivity greater than zero and smaller than the productivity of the worker with the highest productivity.

When I had built and studied some of the features of the solution, I gave a paper at the 1972 summer economics workshop at Stanford. Right in front of me as I spoke were the brilliant Abba Lerner and the master economist Ken Arrow, with whom I had worked at the RAND Corporation years before. I pointed out a provocative implication of the model: the *marginal* tax rate on wage income of the highest earners—the rate at which tax revenue increases with a small increase of taxable income at the highest income level—must be zero for, if it were not, a sufficiently small cut of the marginal rate would increase a little *both* the government's tax revenue and the after-tax income of the highest earner. When I finished, Ken said he could not believe this proposition was right! Then Abba said, "But, Ken, it's like a firm maximizing profit by driving marginal revenue down to marginal cost at which point marginal profit is zero!" Thus, Rawlsian justice does *not* eliminate inequality, however defined; it may decrease it—depending on conditions—or it may increase it. What is crucial is it increases to the maximum the rewards of the workers who are the least advantaged.

The ultimate decline of the marginal tax rate was one finding from the model. Another—obvious on its face—was that the optimum tax policy in the model aims to collect the maximum tax revenue—the realization of so-called taxable capacity. Variants of the initial model were also studied. Of course, conservatives and old-style liberals were opposed to the Rawlsian goal from the outset out of fear that it would mean maximizing tax revenue. This simple model was set out in my paper, "Taxation of Wage Income for Economic Justice," published in August 1973 by the *Quarterly Journal of Economics*.[7] (Some of the methods employed in the analysis had recently been introduced by James Mirrlees in his 1971 paper, "An Exploration in the Theory of Optimum Income Taxation."[8] He had left the door wide open for me to drive through.)

On the face of it, then, it would be an obstruction of Rawlsian justice if the government were to divert any—let alone much—of the revenue raised by taxation of wage income to *other* goals. Instituting free medical care to all, say, might force a sizeable cut in the tax revenue left to finance wage subsidies; even free medical care to working people might cause low-wage workers a net loss of well-being. How would Rawls have responded?

I saw that his book was understood by most if not nearly all essayists invoking his name as a call for huge tax revenue to be spent on all sorts of welfare programs with little or no concern for the least advantaged workers. Rawls's theory of justice is about those participating in society's central project—its economy. I wrote a letter to Jack in mid-April 1976 from Amsterdam urging him to explain again that his theory of justice is about rewarding the work of the least advantaged, not the poor in general. Years went by, though, without any response. At last, he responded in his paper "The Priority of Right and Ideas of the Good," which appeared in *Philosophy and Public Affairs*. In that paper he wrote, "Those who surf all day off Malibu must find a way to support themselves and would not be entitled to public funds."[9] I felt my understanding of *Justice* was vindicated.

Yet several questions surrounding his book must be taken up. For one, it would surely be seen as a step away from Rawls's vision to divert much, let alone most, of the revenue raised by the Rawlsian tax on wage income to the introduction or expansion of social programs for subsidized housing, food, and medical care. Rawls is reported to have been asked how he would propose the institution of justice he envisioned to respond to requests to siphon off some of the tax revenue raised for the least advantaged workers. He is said to have replied that, figuratively speaking, the government ought to ask the working poor whether they would approve of such diversions of their incomes. As a practical matter, of course, many of the hundreds of bills that would call for additional government spending might get past any approval process the working poor might have formed for that purpose. Many government programs sought by a range of wage earners will be seen as good for the working poor, too, and win adoption on that ground.

I would say, although I could not have articulated it in the 1970s—that, just as the concept of justice is fundamental even if no particular conception of it is yet widely agreed upon or even widely studied, so too the concept of an economic system and set of values offering the participants opportunities to pursue the good life or a life well lived is basic. This is the area called "welfare economics." (Scholars in ancient times spoke of the "just and the good.") The establishment of national defense may also be necessary if people are to look to the future—to invest in capital, invest in their education, and ponder possible innovations and new directions. (Adam Smith was not wrong about that.) There are also the matters of safe streets, property rights, and public health. Obviously, public services require government outlays, which for the most part have to be covered sooner or later by tax revenues. A feasible way to finance all this, it would seem, lies in taxing *capital* (leaving aside other property) to fund the *public* services—the costs of the various protections and services—and taxing *wages* to fund the *subsi-dization* of low-wage employment. But what would be the best way to do this?

In an economy with a great many disadvantaged workers, it is conceivable that the best solution involves maximizing the tax revenue from taxation of wage income *plus* profits income. That, however, would leave open whether wage subsides ought to be set equal to exactly the revenue raised by taxation of wage income or by more than that. In the 1970s, I could not answer that question, and I never asked Rawls. Perhaps it is unanswerable.

On rereading some of Rawls's book, however, the way he discusses the idea of justice to the least advantaged workers suggests that the more advantaged workers, bound by their sense of justice, would be glad to see some of whatever pay they choose to earn redistributed to the less advantaged workers. It did not occur to him that the more advantaged savers—savers more able than the others at earning a return on their investment—would be glad to redistribute some of their resulting earnings (from their saving) to the less advantaged savers or to the less-able workers. But, no doubt, the question has not been fully answered.

After my first paper on Rawlsian justice—modeling what that justice would look like in an extremely simple kind of economy—a large part of my work took up for some time questions about a Rawlsian economy with capital, overlapping generations, and some principle for determining the national saving. Fortunately in the mid-1970s, I met Janusz Ordover, a doctoral candidate at Columbia, and soon suggested to him that he join me in a further exploration of this uncharted territory. (Janusz had been a protégé of Polish economic theorist Oskar Lange, originator of market socialism, so I was pleased he also became a protégé of mine.)

The first work coming out of our interchanges was a chapter in his doctoral dissertation, of which I was the adviser, on taxation of wages *and* interest (or profits) in a simple growth model. The published work was his "Distributive Justice and Optimal Taxation of Wages and Interest in a Growing Economy."[10] The next work was our joint journal article, "Linear Taxation of Wealth and Wages for Intergenerational Lifetime Justice: Some Steady-State Cases."[11] It was interesting that going from one model to another may have critical impacts on the optimal structure of taxes for maximization of the lowest wage rates. (A rather different line of work began when, on a visit to Los Angeles, I came into conversation with John Riley at the University of California, Los Angeles, on what a Rawlsian view of intergenerational justice would imply. Our work appears in "Rawlsian Growth: Dynamic Programming of Capital and Wealth for Intergenerational 'Maximin' Justice."[12])

A plan quite different from Rawls's was the universal basic income (UBI) advocated at length by Philippe Van Parijs, a Belgian political philosopher, in his 1995 book *Real Freedom for All: What (if Anything) Can Justify Capitalism?* and revived in the United States by the business owner and political candidate Andrew Yang in 2019.[13] It is important that society understand the adverse consequences of such a plan, so I will address the proposal of Van Parijs—that is, the anti-Rawls view.

Around 1999, at a small gathering convened by Amartya Sen to consider new ideas, held at Trinity College, Cambridge, I encountered Van Parijs. He started things off with his argument for UBI. I was appalled and attacked his proposal with fury, but no one spoke in my support. I was afraid that Amartya and his wife, Emma Rothschild, would not speak to me, but as I was leaving the dinner table, Amartya reached out his hand as if to express his appreciation, even solidarity, with my criticism. Not long after this clash, I was invited by the *Boston Review* to write a response to Van Parijs's article, "A Basic Income for All."[14]

Unfortunately, the institution of a UBI in a country although it would be one way to provide the poor with the income with which to live, would do nothing to pull up wages of low-wage workers so they can *support themselves*—an ability that, in the Western nations at any rate, people generally need for their self-esteem. (A cascade of indirect effects might raise wages a little for a while but would slow the growth of wages over the near future.) UBI would draw people away from work, thus causing them to miss the dignity, sense of belonging, self-respect, self-help, and job satisfaction that come only from work. As I have argued at other opportunities in the past, the UBI would entice people and their children away from meaningful work and thus from a sense of involvement in the economy—society's central project. It is disappointing that UBI has not received widespread opposition.[15]

An objection by some to the standard UBI is the high price tag: If tax revenue is not or cannot be increased, it would necessitate a large cut of other social spending, as Daron Acemoglu argued in a June 2019 essay in *Project Syndicate*, "Why Universal Basic Income Is a Bad Idea."[16] True, low-wage subsidies to the Rawlsian level would have a considerable price tag—all of it born by very-high-wage-income taxpayers in the Rawlsian model I built—yet those disincentives to work at the high end are accompanied by positive incentives to work at the low end. In contrast, a UBI of Van Parijs's proportions, in reducing *all people's* incentives to work—some people's by quite a lot— would evidently cost more, perhaps *a lot* more.

At Columbia in the fall of 1971, I came to appreciate its glorious past. The Faculty House was the locus where one could meet hugely interesting people. Isidor Rabi, one of the physicists involved in the Manhattan Project, and Robert Merton, the great sociologist and a model of originality and breadth, were often around. Jacques Barzun was there too, but I never met him. I soon became friendly with Sidney Morgenbesser, for years a legendary professor of moral philosophy who had extraordinarily broad interests, although he was famously incapable of writing. He and his wife, Joann Haimson, invited me to a New Year's Day party at their apartment where I got to chat with Thomas Kuhn, creator of the notion of a "paradigm shift" in his book *The Structure of Scientific Revolutions*—a notion that fascinated me.[17] These outstanding figures were direct heirs, even students in some cases, of such greats as philosopher John Dewey, statistical theorist Harold Hotelling, literary critic Lionel Trilling, and chemist Harold Urey. In the 1930s, Columbia and Chicago had been ranked at the top.

Three of us—Kelvin Lancaster, Ronald Findlay, and I—went to work to pull up the department to a high standard, and we succeeded spectacularly on the macro side. We were fortunate to recruit Robert Mundell, well known for his work on international trade, the "open-economy macro" (with the famous two-quadrant diagram), and the "supply-side" economics of monetary and fiscal policy. I had telephoned him to express my hopes he would accept the invitation and assure him that his position would not be in the least demanding. Remembering him when he was a student, I recruited Guillermo Calvo to operate on the macroeconomic theory side, and, having met him at Stanford, I recruited John Taylor to handle the econometric side.

Toward the end of the decade, the accomplished macroeconomist Stanley Fischer commented to me that the Columbia department had the best macroeconomics team in the country.

At Columbia in January 1972, I met Viviana Montdor who had taken a job filing exams in a back room next to the copy machine in the Economics Department. For three days, I asked her for a cigarette and on the fourth day invited her to a concert of the New York Philharmonic conducted by Leonard Bernstein. Coming from different backgrounds, we had interesting conversations, and I was impressed by her intelligence and sophistication. She had grown up in Buenos Aires, studied in Paris, and became fluent in Spanish, French, and Italian. We married in October 1974 and moved into an apartment for us and her two children, Monica and Eduardo. Together we set our course. Viviana studied painting and went on to be an interpreter in New York. Our marriage proved to be pivotal in my life. At her urging, we struck out toward Europe. She thought it was important that I got to know other ways of living and to understand societies through exposure to different peoples and their cultures.

The first step was the Summer Conference at the Palazzo in Santa Colomba, near Siena, Italy, where Bob Mundell and his wife Valerie Natsios spent the summers and Paul Volcker was a regular visitor. What fun we had! At the end, a safari piloted by Michael Kuczynski took the five of us to our Tuscan destination, covered with dust.

At the conference, we asked Christian von Weizäcker to let us know if he learned of a visiting position in Europe, and soon he did. We went to Amsterdam in the summer of 1978, where I gave a few lectures at the University of Amsterdam. We also met

Marlies and Jürgen Schröder, who later arranged an invitation to the University of Mannheim over the summers of 1979 and 1980, living in the magical Odenwald, Germany—the forest in the mythic *Ring of the Nibelung*. In these two visits, I assembled my papers and wrote prefaces for *Studies in Macroeconomic Theory: Volume 1, Employment and Inflation* and *Volume 2, Redistribution and Growth*.[18]

These three summer visits were the beginning of two decades of involvement in Europe. Yet Columbia and New York remained the place where I did most, although by no means all, of my thinking and writing.

5

SUPPLY-SIDERS,
"NEW CLASSICALS" AND
AN UN-KEYNESIAN SLUMP

With the microfoundations of macroeconomics laid in the 1960s and Rawlsian foundations for a theory of economic justice developed in the 1970s, I had no backlog of theoretical ideas when the 1980s arrived. There were, however, some phenomena to explain and questions about recent theories to address.

Challenges had piled up to serious levels by the start of the 1980s in much of the West. In the United States, the social unrest that had started in the late 1960s was of high concern throughout the 1970s, as was the outbreak of inflation in the 1970s that followed the collapse of the fixed exchange rate system. Another concern was the slowdown of economic growth, measured in terms of total factor productivity, that had started in the early 1970s (and remains unabated aside for the years during the IT Revolution). In the United States, President Jimmy Carter in his much-discussed televised speech of July 1979 spoke of a *malaise* gripping the nation—a view derided by Ronald Reagan in the following presidential campaign.[1] In Great Britain, the outbreak of an unprecedented number of scandals in the 1970s and 1980s may have been a sign of some loss of spirit. Prime Minister Margaret Thatcher seemed to have sensed such a loss. She has been quoted as saying that "life used to be about trying to do something." What were the responses to any of this?

Viewing America's decade-long slowdown as a result of taxes choking off business investment, President Reagan pushed through Congress legislation aimed at boosting investment through deep cuts in taxation of corporate profits. Viewing Britain's long stagnation as their models did—namely due to the regulations and spending of the welfare state—Thatcher injected a dose of free markets, deregulation, and belt-tightening aimed at encouraging entry of new firms and new industries. The tax cuts were hotly criticized by Democrats and the reforms were bitterly attacked by Labor. In both countries, observers poured over the data on investment and growth to test the claims being made for the cuts and the reforms.

Generally speaking, economists were caught having little idea of what an optimal economic policy toward the slowdown, or stagnation, was—and what the costs and benefits would have been. At this stage of my development in macroeconomics and welfare economics, I had rather little idea myself. Oddly, hardly anyone was working in this area.

A WALK ON THE SUPPLY SIDE

Enter Robert Mundell. Bob and I had met in late December 1959 during the annual meeting of the American Economic Association at an informal reception hosted by the National Science Foundation. Bob was nine months older than I and had gained more ground in obtaining his doctorate a year faster. More important, his blockbuster paper, "The Monetary Economics of International Adjustment under Fixed and Flexible Exchange Rates," was to come out the following May in the

Quarterly Journal of Economics.[2] We found we had some shared interests. I asked him what he was working on at the time. He said he was working on inflation and real interest rates, and I said I had just written a paper on that subject.

Mundell's main contribution in that stage of his career—from my perspective, at any rate—was his extension in that May 1960 paper of Keynesian employment theory to an open economy. In that paper, he showed that John Hicks's mathematization— his investment-saving and liquidity preference–money supply (IS-LM) model determining interest rate and output— of Keynes's theory of a closed economy could be expanded to describe a *small* open economy. In this model, market forces operate to keep the interest rate in this economy equal to the world interest rate: the *total* demand, domestic and foreign, for the country's output must be just enough to pull up the country's interest rate to the level of the world rate. And it is this interest rate that governs, or determines, the country's output and employment. So, an increase of *domestic* demand does *not* pull up output and employment. "Where did the demand go?" Bob loved to ask rhetorically. "It went overseas!" he explained. Fiscal stimulus, then, does not work in this setting.

Yet *monetary* stimulus does work. An increase in the supply of money forces output to rise until the interest rate is pulled back to the world level. When teaching macroeconomics to undergraduates, I always liked to show Hicks's diagram with just the LM curve and a horizontal line given by the world interest rate. I then ask the students to "discuss." The best students see the diagram as showing, in that setting, that domestic investment and saving—the IS curve—have no impact.

Bob's model was broadened a decade later. His graduate school adviser, Charlie Kindleberger, invited me to a 1969 conference of the International Economic Association in Portugal's

Algarve to be the discussant of a paper of Bob's, "Monetary Relations between Europe and America."[3] In this paper, he went a step beyond the small economy model having an exogenous world interest rate. The model described two large economies jointly determining their common interest rate. For the first time, we were shown how increased investment demand in one of the countries pulls up the countries' shared interest rate, thus stimulating output and employment in *that* economy, while contracting investment in the *other* country's economy.

Bob was to have another impact—one quite consequential in the United States. In the largely prosperous decades after the war, fears of a "liquidity trap"—the problem that interest rates were so low they could not be reduced further by the central bank—had abated, so that aggregate demand could be managed through either fiscal stimulus *or* monetary stimulus. For years and years, Keynesians had not come to agree on whether, in a large economy—one large enough to be effectively a closed economy—a slump ought to be treated with monetary stimulus applied by the central bank or by fiscal stimulus applied by the treasury.

Mundell's insight, deriving no doubt from his background in trade theory, was that the fiscal tool has a "comparative advantage" over the monetary tool in one respect, while the monetary tool has such an advantage in another respect. An implication, he showed, was that the *fiscal* tool—setting the size of the budget deficit (or surplus)—ought to be assigned to stabilization of the employment level, while the *monetary* tool—setting the benchmark interest rate—would be assigned to stabilization of the price level. Reversing that assignment, he argued, would lead to a futile attempt to (1) stabilize prices by more and more fiscal tightening and (2) stabilize output by more and more monetary stimulus, thus triggering hyperinflation and depression. He noted more than once that the U.S. Council of Economic

Advisers, following what he called the "Samuelson-Tobin 'neo-classical synthesis,'" had advocated low interest rates to spur growth and a budget surplus to siphon off excess liquidity and thus curb inflation—a policy Bob thought would drive the economy off the rails.[4]

This was a remarkable departure from then-standard macro-economic thinking and a remarkably influential one at that. He was awarded the 1999 Nobel Prize—the whole of it—for "his analysis of monetary and fiscal policy" more than anything else. Yet this work changed the practice of fiscal policy around the world. I would wager that, if he ever looked back at his career, it was the thrill he must have felt in the years around 1980 as he sought to get his policy adopted in Washington, DC, and abroad that was most memorable.

With his arrival at Columbia in the fall of 1974, Bob began to meet regularly with a group seeking to formulate a supply-side policy to combat low employment. A good-size group of economists, which I often joined, convened annually at his summer home outside Siena, Italy, to present their ideas. When in 1980 Ronald Reagan won the presidency in a landslide and set about to persuade the Congress to enact the massive cut of tax rates on corporate profits (and some other incomes to a lesser extent), supply-side economics became a fascination of the general public, and Bob became a public figure. (In a 1984 issue of the *New Yorker*, Bob was the subject of a huge interview on his supply-side economics.[5] In my mind, the magazine had put Bob right up there with its pieces on John J. McCloy after reviving post-war Germany and Ted Williams after that last great day in Fenway Park.)

Yet new policies bring uncertainty—opposition too—and the Mundell policy mix was certainly something new. The stated policy left it unclear where the economy was going, what path the capital stock would take, and where the price level would land. Furthermore, adherence to that supply-side policy mix might return the economy to a growth path that people don't want. (The supply-side math—all equations in the rates of change, not levels—does not let us choose the end-points, or better, choose the equilibrium growth path we want the supply-side policy to connect with.)

I had another concern. As Bob later emphasized in his Nobel Prize Lecture, "supply-side economics . . . was based on a policy mix that delivered price stability through monetary discipline and stimulation of employment and growth [through fiscal means]."[6] To boost demand, the monetary authority is to bring down actual and expected rates of inflation to a desirable level; and to boost supply, the fiscal authority is to reduce tax rates on profits to boost corporations' investment demand—or contract public expenditure to boost the supply of saving. Thus, either way, the policy mix pushes the capital stock onto a higher growth path, but it does so at the cost of pushing the public debt onto a higher path. As Paul Samuelson said, "with proper fiscal and monetary policies, our economy can have full employment and whatever rate of capital formation it wants."[7]

But there may be a problem. When the government—starting with a balanced budget, say—embarks on such an operation to steepen the climb of the capital stock, the injection of the public debt (or more debt than what was there at the start) creates a *wedge* between wealth and capital. As a result, the decline of interest rates—thus the rise of wage rates—is slowed down by the drip-drip rise of the wedge between capital and wealth caused by the oozing expansion of the public debt.

In the United States, however, the Reagan administration seemed to believe that tax rates on corporate profits could remain greatly reduced for any length of time to sustain elevated rates of investment, and thus faster growth of the capital stock. The accompanying rise of the public debt operates to dash such a belief, however. Yet that was not understood at the time—nor is it understood now.

Much might be said—for or against—the supply-side idea. Clearly, a huge cut in tax rates on profits can be expected to bring only a one-time climb of the capital stock onto a higher time path—not any sustained increase of the growth rate. There is also the cost. A sustained cut of the tax rates on profits would have to be financed somehow. Regaining the tax revenue being lost by lower tax rates on *profits* through higher tax rates on *wage income* would be problematic if those tax rates are already set very high to meet social needs. In this case, crimping the supply of labor to boost the supply of capital might be undesirable for most if not all participants in the economy.

When Bob and I met over lunch one day in the 1980s to talk about his supply-side thesis, I brought up the point that a sustained fiscal deficit would leave the economy with a swollen public debt, and that, in adding to people's wealth relative to national income, it would squeeze national saving relative to national income. Thus, ultimately, it would *decrease* the capital stock relative to national output. For me, that put in question the supply-side thesis that a deficit-financed cut in profit rates would have the net effect of shifting up the path of the capital stock.

Bob said only, "All those bonds." I couldn't tell whether he thought I had a point.[8] (He often liked to be enigmatic.)

Of course, the proof of the pudding is in the evidence of what followed the Reagan tax cuts. There was indeed an economic recovery over the 1980s, but there would have been the expectation of recovery from the shocks of the 1970s—the oil shocks, the currency changes, and violence on the streets—even without any tax cut. (Did investment expenditure rise more or even as much as consumption expenditure? No. The share of investment in GDP appears to have exhibited a downward trend through the 1980s, while the share of consumption expenditure exhibited an upward trend.) More evidence came with the Trump tax cuts. In the years 2017–2019, the economy went from prosperity to boom, but investment did not increase proportionately more than consumption did.

THE NEW CLASSICAL SCHOOL

In macroeconomic theory, the importance of expectations for understanding wage, price, and employment dynamics had been quickly accepted in the 1980s. The theory that I began in the latter half of the 1960s—that when business weakens, a firm won't cut its prices or wages much (or at all) if it expects the other firms won't cut theirs much (so wages adjust slowly if at all)— had gained adherents from the start. After all, Keynesians had no reason not to accept this microfoundation—although some saw it as heresy—and it was sometimes called New Keynesian economics.

Yet what came to be called the New Classical school—the school of thought arising at the University of Chicago—also began to gain adherents in the 1970s. In those years, three papers by Robert Lucas, leader of the school, supposed that firms as well as individuals have what John Muth had dubbed "rational expectations"—that the expectations acquired by individuals and firms are the expectations that could be calculated from analysis of a sound, mathematical model. This postulate leaves no room for the premise that firms, in setting their price or wages for the quarter or the year, will systematically underestimate the price or wage cuts to be made by the other firms—thus causing them to cut their own prices or wages less than they would have had they been fully informed. (Ironically, in the first of these papers, Lucas built on the parable of an "islands economy" that appeared in my introduction to the *Microfoundations* volume.[9])

I previously had delved into Frank Knight's 1921 *Risk, Uncertainty, and Profit*; Keynes's 1921 *A Treatise on Probability* and his 1937 article "The General Theory of Unemployment"; and Friedrich Hayek's 1948 *Individualism and Economic Order*, but I was unable to get into Lucas's way of thinking.

I could agree that if a firm were to observe year after year the extent to which other firms reacted to the sorts of shocks they were accustomed to experiencing, then this firm might soon start learning about these reactions, and sooner or later, adjust its own reactions accordingly. In the world of New Classical economics, however, all such learning has already taken place and the underlying forces are already known to all the firms. In the real world, I maintain, a nation's economy is not generally on an equilibrium path characterized by correct (at least unbiased) expectations and, barring new developments, it is in the process of learning the correct expectations as the economy evolves. All this and much more was set out in the 1983 volume, *Individual Forecasting and Aggregate Outcomes: "Rational Expectations" Examined*, which came out of the conference Roman Frydman, a like-minded advocate of modern economics and longtime friend, and I organized at New York University.[10] Of special interest to me were two essays by Roman, the essay by Margaret Bray discussed by Roy Radner, and the paper by Juan Carlos di Tata. Roman and I were not alone in our thinking.

I concluded that Lucas and his collaborators showed that with the premise of Muth's "rational expectations," one could arrive at some interesting results. Their work, however, does not disprove that, in a world of Knightian uncertainty (an uncertainty hugely heightened by new forces of change) price and wage setters make their decisions using guesswork or hunches as to what others will decide to do. In contrast, the microeconomic foundations of the late 1960s *do* appear to offer a useful theory of short-term business fluctuations.

This was my introduction to the theory wars. In the 1880s, there had been such a war between the focus of Gustav Schmoller's German Historical School on historical studies and the focus of Carl Menger's Austrian school on economic theory—the famous *Methodenstreit*. Theory won, thanks to the fundamental advances of the neoclassical school founded by Léon Walras, Alfred Marshall, and Knut Wicksell. In the 1920s and 1930s, another such war broke out when the neoclassical school, led then by Joseph Schumpeter, Irving Fisher, and Arthur Pigou, was increasingly overshadowed by the modernist theorists, Frank Knight, Keynes, and Hayek. This development was similar to what occurred in philosophy with the rise of William James and Henri Bergson a decade or two earlier. My work in the 1960s on the formation of expectations on which to build a micro-macro theory and the further contributions at the ensuing microfoundations conference in January 1969 constituted a new body of micro-macro theory that might best be called new modern—with Knight, Keynes, and Hayek being the *first* modernists.

The work of Lucas and others in the 1970s built the micro-macro theory often called New Classical. They bravely extended the classical theory to economies regularly disturbed by fluctuations governed by known probabilities and would go no further than the essentially classical world. Of course, I was interested in the results they obtained. But I believed that, in general, to suppose that the expectations of the actors in the model are "rational" (and thus based on the very same model that the analyst has adopted and perhaps conceived) would be so unrealistic as to make it dangerous to rely on the results from that model. I was grateful to be able to work in the world of Knight, Keynes, and Hayek.

I was saddened to hear the New Classicals insinuated that theorists like me and others, with our recognition of the marked uncertainty and imperfect information in the economy, had created a set of models about how the economy works that are less sophisticated and, as a result, not descriptive—or at least less descriptive than their models. Hence, they seemed to think that other theories could safely be discarded in favor of the classical view in their models. As I saw it, the New Classicals, with their adherence to "rational expectations," showed they had little or no sense of a modern economy—an economy that, at its core, is driven by the judgment, intuitions, and imagination of a modern people.

Importantly, however, the New Classical school was coming to be dominant in the teaching of economic theory and the thinking in many policymaking circles across most of the United States. Rainer Masera, who had studied at Oxford, told me recently that John Hicks, whose simple IS-LM model had made it possible to grasp Keynes's theory, had become furious over the wide acceptance of New Classical economics. (According to Rainer, Hicks thought I was the "only one" in the United States opposing it.)

I and others have continued to find that the editors of the economic academic journals are loathe to publish pieces that adopt premises and draw conclusions that are inimical or foreign to the thinking that has come to be in vogue and considered the most scientific thinking. The serious cost of this mindset is that it blocks the airing of new theories, thus slowing progress in the field and discouraging the creation of new theories—hence, perpetuating present-day thought, no matter how inadequate and misguided it may be. At the 2018 Global Solutions Conference held in Berlin, I happened upon a panel in which George Akerlof made a presentation deploring the takeover of the economic journals by the leaders of prevailing economic thought—James Heckman has also spoken on this subject.[11] From the floor, I expressed my own long disgruntlement with this state of affairs.

WRITING *POLITICAL ECONOMY*

While keeping up on the supply-side debate and catching up with the New Classical papers, I worked over the first half of the 1980s almost entirely on writing a textbook. I was under contract with W. W. Norton to prepare an introductory textbook in economics, and I had delayed getting started for more than a decade. (Donald Lamm, the chair and great friend, told me one day that the board meetings began with the authors of the most overdue manuscripts, and I had risen to second place—behind Shirley MacLaine.)

Certainly, the time was right for a new text. Paul Samuelson's *Economics*, the reigning introductory textbook, was first published in 1946—almost four decades before I was writing my book. His book contained brilliant expositions of matters central to those times, notably employment determination. But economics had developed enormously in those four decades. I felt it was important to offer college students a more up-to-date and broader introduction to economics.

It was a daunting undertaking, especially since I wanted to do it right. For me, that meant micro first, then the market economy, "economic justice," micro-macro, and other exciting developments. "These basic matters," the preface explains, "lay the ground for the main subjects in political economy—the choice of economic systems and public laws, the policies that society has available for coordinating and rewarding its members' participation in the economy."[12] The book focuses on the debate between the classical defenders of the market and the postclassical critics of the market, who argue for extensive government intervention to replace or repair its defects. It also gives clear discussions of the New Classical and New Keynesian schools on monetary economics and employment fluctuations.

I made occasional departures from conventional thinking. One departure was on nonpecuniary rewards: "It would be difficult to underestimate the importance of nonpecuniary rewards. . . . To create something, anything, . . . [is] of great value to virtually all of us," as Gunnar Myrdal noted.[13]

Another departure of mine was on work. Most people would not want a life without work, so for them work is a source of "utility," as the independent thinkers Thorsten Veblen and Alfred Marshall understood. Yet another departure from textbooks was an entire chapter on Rawls's fairness as well as the equalitarianism of Bernard Shaw and Richard Tawney, and the utilitarianism of Jeremy Bentham.

Creation of the textbook could be said to have begun in 1979 when I taught an experimental version of an introductory course in economics. Writing began January 1980 in Buenos Aires and Rio de Janeiro, continued over three summers in Mannheim and Munich, and ended in Fiesole and New York in the summer of 1984.

When turning over the manuscript to Norton toward the end of summer, I saw that in the chapter titled "The Gains from Cooperation" (mostly on the gains from trade and comparative advantage), I had not brought up an aspect that was bothering me: the impact of a country's foreign trade on distribution (i.e., wage rates and the rest). "Ricardo left unexplored a thorny issue," I wrote, "Would all the Portuguese who were engaged in the production of cloth gain from the opening of foreign trade? Would all the English in the wine-growing business be better off?"[14] The analysis fascinated me, and I spent months with it, delaying the publication even further. (A colleague, Robert Feenstra, went further with this subject.)

The book was adopted in a few schools, most of them in Europe, including the Stockholm School of Economics, where it was used for years by Lars Bergman, and the University of Amsterdam, where Erik Bartelsman, who had been my assistant when creating it, long championed it. It also got into the Economics Tripos Part I at Cambridge, Erasmus University in Rotterdam, and the Institut d'Etudes Politique de Paris (in a superb translation by the French economist Jacques Le Cacheux). But it was not used widely. In the United States, economics teachers regarded it as pretentious or difficult. That was painful, of course.

Yet, it didn't really matter. The book was not intended to familiarize a large number of college graduates with the features of the contemporary economy. It was more an anthology of the marvelous advances in the field called political economy, or simply economics, and—for me—the text was an expression of how gratifying it was to be a participant in its development. The four-year project was a labor of love.

When my first copy reached me in mid-June at the Banca d'Italia, I couldn't resist taking a break from time to time to read snatches of it. I was pleased to find that it was much appreciated by some scholars whose opinion mattered to me most. In a handwritten letter—unfortunately, lost in an office mishap— John Rawls had nothing but praise for it. Jim Tobin was said to have remarked in a session on textbooks at the 1986 annual meeting of the American Economic Association that it was the best textbook since Irving Fisher's *Elementary Principles of Economics* published in 1912. The book remains a source of some pride.

THE WORK IN ROME AND FIESOLE

In 1985–86, I was on sabbatical (a Guggenheim), and my first stop was a half year as visiting scholar at the Banca d'Italia. I had met Luigi Spaventa at a conference in Sao Paolo, and subsequently he had told Tommaso Padoa-Schioppa, then the number two at the Bank of Italy—and soon to spearhead Italy's joining the euro—that I would be receptive to an invitation. (Luigi and his wife Clare Royce were to become good friends, as were Tommaso and his wife, the economist Fiorella Kostoris.)

The timing was awful in one respect. The murderous Red Brigades was at peak strength. They had recently kidnapped and killed former Prime Minister Aldo Moro in Florence and, just weeks before I arrived, they had assassinated the economist Ezio Tarantelli in the parking lot behind the Bank. He and I had been looking forward to arguing with each other on some matter or other. When I arrived there in mid-June, security at the Bank was by far the tightest I had ever seen. A year or so later, a hit list was found that included some economists.

Rome was at its most glorious, however. We lived in the quarter called Parioli on Via Paisiello, which was not far from the park Villa Borghese and the Hotel Parco dei Principi where the International Econometric Society held its first World Congress in 1965. I had stayed overnight in Parioli on my tour of Europe in 1952, but life there seemed to have changed. One could feel the energy in the people. I saw a young woman exploding out of a shop onto her motorcycle and speed away. In the string of outdoor restaurants along the winding Viale Rossini the talk was lively and happy.

Yet the country was in a slump, and so was the entire European Economic Community (EEC). In Italy, the unemployment rate had risen to 12.8 percent in 1985–1986 from 5.7 percent in 1974–1979 (and 1960–1967, too). In the nine countries of the EEC, unemployment had reached about 11 percent in 1985–1986 from 4.6 percent in 1974–1979. This was a *big* downturn, one not seen again until the Global Financial Crisis of 2007–2009. (Interestingly, under Thatcher, unemployment reached 12.1 percent from 4.3 percent—not much worse than in Italy and the EEC. Maybe her policies and decisions, as a whole, had not been the cause of the bad decade in Britain.)

In contrast, the unemployment rate in the United States rose little—to around 7.0 percent in 1985–1986 from around 6.8 percent in 1974–1979 (and 5 percent in 1960–1967). It may be worth noting that the unemployment rate briefly rose to 9.6 percent in 1982–1983 before falling back to 7.5 percent in 1984.

Ultimately, then, one could say that as the United States was pulling out of its 1970s slump, Europe was going from its two decades of prosperity starting in the 1960s *into* its 1980s slump. For Keynesians, the opposite direction taken by Europe just added to the puzzle. (In Keynesian theory, "a rising tide lifts all boats," as John Kennedy liked to say. Hence, it predicted the U.S. recovery would lift Europe, not sink it!) I wondered: What events and mechanisms could shed light on the slump in Europe amidst the recovery in the United States?

Being in Rome, and at the Banca d'Italia no less, I was in a good place to think about this puzzle. Stefano Micossi taught me much about the Italian economy, and, when I wanted to research something, Luigi Guiso and Lorenzo Bini Smaghi were ready to render research assistance. In Rome, Luigi Spaventa, Marcello De Cecco, and Giovanni Tria, all of Sapienza University, were good friends.

The observations and data on Europe that I noticed did not indicate any domestic shock important enough to be the cause of its serious downturn. There was an external shock, however, one of a rather large size: the passage of the 1981 Reagan tax cut on corporate profits. The degree of stimulus to investment demand over the 1980s brought by this tax cut—first the anticipation of it, then the realization—was much discussed in financial circles.

The theory of such a result was familiar Keynesian fare among economists in those times. In a two-country world with a floating exchange rate, a rise of investment demand in county A—such as the rise brought by a cut in the profits tax—creates an excess demand there, which forces an appreciation of its currency, and thus a currency *depreciation* in country B. The latter development brings about in country B an increase of its export demand, and thus an *increase* of aggregate demand and employment there. In short, the rise of aggregate demand at home, in causing an excess of demand there, raises world interest rates, thus cutting investment and jobs abroad.

I wondered whether there might be some *other* channel through which America's tax cut on its profits had a negative impact on Europe? In continental Europe, I knew, there was a tendency among many economists to look to some version of classical economics—economic theory from Wicksell and Fisher in the early 1900s to Pigou and Ramsey in the 1920s and early 1930s—for an explanation of Europe's slump. I understood that, in classical theory, if the productivity of labor fell behind its equilibrium path—the path expected when real wage increases were negotiated—unemployment would rise above *its* expected path, causing employment to fall or, at any rate, to slow. But I had no immediate idea of what might have caused a decrease in the demand for labor in Europe.

Imaginably, some other species of Keynesian theory might explain the slump in Europe. For example, could America's tax cut (and the anticipation of it), in driving up the world real rate of interest, have dampened investment demand, and thus employment too, in the rest of the world, Europe included? Those economies had not enjoyed a tax cut that would more than offset the interest rate rise. (One could speculate on this matter without feeling un-Keynesian.)

Toward the end of my time at the Bank of Italy, I began to think along the recent lines of the customer market model developed in a joint paper with Sidney Winter for the 1969 conference and published in the *Microeconomic Foundations* volume—although this thinking did not produce a paper at the Bank.[15]

That September was marked by a new horizon not far off and some long good-byes. I saw that I would be coming back to Rome the next summer—and possibly for many summers after that. In the spring, Giovanni Tria, in a visit at Columbia, had told me there was interest in my visiting at a second university in Rome expected to open the following year, and Luigi Paganetto, who was to build the Economics Department, had soon confirmed that interest. He later drove me out to what would become the University of Rome Tor Vergata, walked me through the dusty foundations, and introduced me to President Enrico Garaci.

Viviana and I gave a big party to say *addio* to our many Roman friends: Tomasso and Fiorella, Luigi Spaventa and Clare, Stefano Micossi and Daniela, Luigi Paganetto and Stefania, Marcello De Cecco and Julia, and many others. Late in the party, Marcello opened his guitar and enlisted me to sing "Nessun Dorma." Tomasso—one of the fathers of the euro—pulled me aside to tell me why he believed that the euro would be a godsend for Italy, which had been suffering from distracting bouts of inflation for decades. (Some advocates saw the euro as moving investment out of low-return economies to high-return ones, which could have had an ill effect on Italy.)

Leaving the Bank in October 1985, I began a nearly year-long visit at the European University Institute (IUE)—a sort of Shangri-La for scholars in the social sciences—situated in Fiesole, up the long hill from Florence. I promptly got back to the challenge of understanding how the United States might have caused Europe's slump. This led to many exchanges with Jean-Paul Fitoussi, a frequent figure there when not in Paris teaching at Sciences Po and directing the sister institution, French Economic Observatory (OFCE), whom I had gotten to know in my summer visit to IUE and Fiesole.

Thinking more about the paper on "customer markets" that Sid Winter and I wrote in 1969, I began to see that the Reagan tax cut brought a shock to Europe both by raising the real interest rates faced by European firms and—by appreciating the dollar—boosting U.S. competitors' prices (in euros). Both developments induced many European firms to raise their markups, thus contracting output and employment. In the paper that Jean-Paul and I presented at the Brookings conference of June 1986, we argued the following:

> The policy shocks in America had impacts in Europe upon the markup in customer markets, the real price of investment goods output, and the demand for capital . . . These effects in turn had serious repercussions on European employment. . . . The real rate of interest expected by firms was perhaps the major channel here. . . . The rise of real interest rates around 1981–82 to record-setting levels in both the United States and Europe . . . can be attributed largely to the American fiscal stimulus, especially the new investment subsidies. . . . The sharp elevation of actual and, presumably, of expected real interest rates, we argue, induced firms in Europe to widen their markups since it increased the opportunity cost of "investing" in greater or maintained market

share through restraint in present prices at a sacrifice in present cash flow. There being no important demand stimulus to offset it, the result of the price push was a fall of employment in Europe.[16]

Over the next academic year, 1986–1987, Jean-Paul and I worked hard—and with great pleasure—to write a little book, *The Slump in Europe*, brought out in 1988 by a small Oxford publisher, Basil Blackwell. Although the book was not widely read, the thesis was coming to be assimilated among macroeconomists. More important, Jean-Paul and I became the closest of friends and remained so until his sudden death on April 15, 2022. With our annual visits to Paris, Viviana and I became virtually members of Annie and Jean-Paul's family.

Another step in my journey as an economic theorist had been taken. After supplying some microfoundations for Keynes, I had taken an un-Keynesian step without throwing the Keynes-Hicks-Tobin book away.

Above all, I had come up with a surprising idea before the 1980s were out. I had regained my confidence as an economic theorist. On a bus leaving a conference at Guangzhou on the coast of China, I noticed Amartya Sen was sitting alone. We chatted and he asked me about my recent research. I remarked—with some feeling—that I had been worried for some time that after the long immersion in my textbook I wasn't going to have any more new ideas. Amartya had a big laugh. "Only you would think that!"

In fact, I was already onto another new idea: If nonmonetary forces such as tax rates and real prices such as the real interest rate were at work in driving up unemployment in Europe, might a wider set of real forces and real channels operate to cause increased or decreased unemployment? I found myself onto the new hypothesis—structural slumps.

6

A REVOLUTIONARY DECADE

The 1990s were a welcome decade—challenging and constructive. The fall of the Soviet Union brought both an end to the Cold War and fundamental reform to much of eastern Europe. The Information and Technology (IT) Revolution and the birth of the internet era raised hopes that these advances would return the West to rapid growth—growth of total factor productivity (TFP). The lingering slump in Europe was a warning that a lot might be missing in our understanding of unemployment determination. And the continuing spectacle of pitifully low wages among the least advantaged raised the question of whether something might be done about it.

TRANSFORMING EASTERN EUROPE'S ECONOMIES

The fall of communist rule and rise of democratic governments—starting around August 1989 in Poland, Hungary, and Czechoslovakia; then in East Germany with the dramatic fall of the Berlin Wall in November 1989; and in Russia with the emergence of a democratic state aimed at something nearer to a market economy after the crumbling of the Soviet Union by Christmas 1991—constituted one of the most significant developments in economic history. For me, an economist raised and based in the United States—a country where Truman's fiscal surpluses, Nixon's going off gold, and Reagan's tax cuts were perhaps the high points—this was the most exciting governmental development I had ever witnessed.

Little did I know that I would soon have some role, however small, in what unfolded. In July 1990, a group of national leaders from Western nations met in Houston, Texas. They called on a quadrumvirate of international institutions—the International Monetary Fund (IMF), the Organisation for Economic Cooperation and Development (OECD) in Paris, the World Bank (IBRD), and the nascent European Bank for Reconstruction and Development (EBRD)—to form teams of experts to meet Russians active in the reorganization of the national economy. At the request of Jacques Attali, head of the EBRD, Jean-Paul Fitoussi and those he recruited—Ken Arrow, John Flemming, Philippe Aghion, and me—constituted the new bank's mission to Moscow in September. Boarding the nonstop flight from New York's Kennedy Airport to Moscow was a thrill I never forgot.

It was fascinating to hear the Russians meeting with us talk about the plans that were developing and to feel their energy. We were impressed at a meeting in which one of them spoke to us with enormous force about his aims and what he saw were the obstacles to be surmounted. "Now we can have an idea," Ken exclaimed, "how extraordinary the revolutionaries overthrowing the Czar must have been." While the restructuring of Russia's economy was being planned, much of Russian life continued as usual. In our night off, we went to the Bolshoi Theater to see a fine performance of Mussorgsky's great opera, *Boris Godunov*—Ken's favorite. Ultimately, our report to the EBRD was folded into a larger report sent to President George H. W. Bush and other heads of state behind the initiative.

In the fall of 1990, most of us on the task force were absorbed in the newly created Scientific Council of the EBRD, which had added János Kornai, Assar Lindbeck, Luigi Spaventa, and Christian von Weizsäcker. Ken and I were asked to prepare a paper on the rewards to a nation of choosing a capitalist organization for the economy provided there is adequate redistribution and competition. This paper was to be part of the contribution of the EBRD to the Joint Study of the Economy of the Soviet Union requested by the governments of the G–7 and to be released in February 1991.[1]

The paper started with the view that "every economy . . . [is a] system for transmitting information among those making decisions affecting the allocation of the economy's resources"—a view dear to Ken and sufficient for our purposes, but far too narrow a description of the capitalist economies in Britain by the early nineteenth century and in the United States by the mid-nineteenth century.[2] We first took up the role of *marketization*—property rights and what the reformers aptly called price liberalization (which raised monopoly issues)—that is, the scope for a market economy. (Russia's Shatalin Plan envisioned "70 percent of the economy was to be wrested from the central government control and subjected to the discipline of the market."[3])

We then went on to the importance of "privatization, properly regulated." We wrote: "There seem to be no doubts in Soviet minds about the advantageousness of private ownership of small enterprises. One can credit Soviet economists with an appreciation that property such as an apartment or a truck or the business of a restaurant is better looked after if in the hands of a private owner who will pay the consequences of careless management."[4] Yet, we continued: "There seems to be little appreciation of the theoretical merits of having the ownership of an enterprise under the effective control of some bloc of shares belonging to one private owner or coalition of private owners."[5]

Of course, all this was about capitalism—without using the word. I had read Ludwig von Mises's brilliant and witty attack on the alternative to capitalism in his 1922 book *Socialism* and Friedrich Hayek's stolid criticism of corporatism in his 1944 book *The Road to Serfdom*. I had no qualms then calling for the adoption of a capitalist organization of the economies of Eastern Europe. I hadn't been sure about Ken, but I needn't have worried. Although he and I had differed over my work on taxation for economic justice and differed somewhat on altruism, we hit it off on capitalism—"properly regulated" and, of course, properly taxed.

Thinking about capitalism was to be an occupation in the next academic year. In August 1992, I took a yearlong consultant position at the new headquarters of the EBRD working largely as editor of an annual report for the newly created economics department, headed by the Oxford economist, John Flemming. My chief responsibility was to write a paper on the restructuring of the economies of eastern Europe. I imagined that all of us at the bank were interested in helping people in eastern Europe to see the merits of converting their economies into well-functioning capitalism, but perhaps not all of us knew all the standard arguments. Even an explicit definition of capitalism was not widely agreed upon.

In a chat with Leszek Balcerowicz—the towering figure in instituting elements of capitalism into Poland's economy—I asked him what he saw to be at the heart of capitalism. He exclaimed, "Capital is king!" I supposed he meant that, under capitalism, suppliers of capital select the enterprises, with their investments in innovation and expansion, and thus, in a sense, set the economy's heading—its compass direction, so to speak, however far the winds are blowing it off course. That is true in a sense, although owners of capital can succeed only if they march to the beat of consumers. It became clear to me, however, that it is not possible nor necessary to specify all the forces, activities, and connections going on in economies called capitalist. In a way, Leszek, with his exuberance, was expressing the exuberance at the heart of a buoyant capitalist economy. The "spirit" in Max Weber's *The Protestant Ethic and the Spirit of Capitalism* appears to have been more subdued, but Weber too knew that the success of a capitalist economy—even the most basic sort of success (such as keeping up with Schumpeterian opportunities)—required the "zeal" of the participants (to use Gustav Cassel's apt term).

This paper of mine for the EBRD was written over more than a year with the countless input and advice of others and was completed soon before I left the bank in August 1993 to return home. Then the story took a strange turn. I had been back in New York for some time and on a sabbatical at the Russell Sage Foundation when John Flemming phoned me from the bank to say that a meeting was in progress to weigh approval of the various contributions to the first annual report. The vice president was calling for dropping my contribution from the report on the grounds that the bank ought not to take a position on capitalism. After I had conveyed my indignation, John, who was also consternated, had the idea of making my report an *appendix* to the Annual Review—even though that placement made no sense.[6] I agreed and then the bank's committee approved the relocation of my contribution. This unexpected development made me wonder whether the notions in political economy in continental Europe were far more diverse than I would have guessed.

It was hard to leave my paradise in London, even harder than it had been in August 1966. Viviana and I lived in South

Kensington, where with my key to the park in Onslow Square I jogged regularly; we shopped at Harrods and enjoyed the nearby pizza joints and a splendid restaurant long gone. John Flemming and his wife invited us to Oxford where after lunch we walked for hours with the economist Ian Little—a modest man, an insightful economist, and one of the handful of Spitfire and gyrocopters pilots (the pilots about whom Churchill said, "Never was so much owed by so many to so few") who fought off German aircraft in World War II. On my sixtieth birthday, July 26, Viviana organized a smallish dinner at the Dorchester. As we gathered with our guests at the balcony to watch the sunset just after a rain shower, a magnificent rainbow arched across Hyde Park. I couldn't help thinking: though life had been extraordinarily good to me, maybe the best was yet to come.

STRUCTURAL MECHANISMS BEHIND UNEMPLOYMENT RATES

With the approach of the 1990s, I was drawn back to macroeconomics. The draw was not only the "slump in Europe"—not explained by the Keynes–Hicks closed-economy model nor by the Keynesian Mundell–Fleming open-economy model.[7] I felt that there was a whole world of nonmonetary forces—structural shifts and changes in real conditions—acting on the path of the unemployment rate but not through aggregate demand. It was time to widen our perspective on macroeconomic activity.

I had never doubted and don't doubt now the huge truth in the Keynesian thesis: A cut of aggregate demand acts to push unemployment up and a lift of aggregate demand acts to pull unemployment down, other things constant—*ceteris paribus*, as the Romans would have said. Far from having ever denied the plausibility of Keynesian theory, I had contributed a micro-theoretical underpinning to it: When aggregate demand falls, a typical firm would not risk making a cut in its wage scales in the absence of information on whether its competitors in its labor market were going to cut their wages—a situation that came to be called "imperfect information." (Keynes had merely appealed to the downward "stickiness" of money wages and the upward stickiness of money prices.[8]) If I had not approved of all of the policy proposals promoted in part on the ground that they would stimulate "demand," then it was not that I had become a skeptic about the possibility of deficient demand. (Keynes himself seemed to have become agitated by policy proposals that proponents had apparently sought to defend on Keynesian grounds—proposals that Keynes did not subscribe to. In the last months of his life, he wrote in the June 1946 *Economic Journal* of "modernist stuff gone wrong and turned sour and silly."[9])

Throughout the 1970s and 1980s, I had continued to regard that micro-macro work of mine as my peak—the most important of my papers up to that time. (My customer market paper with Sid Winter and my optimal saving paper with Bob Pollak, from the 1960s, also became important.) But no matter how important they were, nothing in these papers required a great deal of theoretical imagination—an exercise of real creativity. They presented a few new observations and insights on a nation's economy, which was most gratifying. But they presented no new big picture of a nation's economy, such as those conceived by Léon Walras, Eugen von Böhm-Bawerk, Joseph Schumpeter, Knut Wicksell, Frank Knight, Frank Ramsey, and Keynes. Economists used to conceive a new view of the economy—to add to the others or to displace some of them. (I can't help commenting that these figures were not ancients: My teacher William Fellner clearly studied Böhm-Bawerk, my friend Paul

Samuelson was Schumpeter's student, and George Stigler, who knew me and my work, was Knight's student.)

In the dawning of the 1990s, however, I made what felt like a pretty big step—developing a structuralist view standing in contrast to the Keynesian view—while not doubting that we can take both views. The slump in Europe over the 1980s—the un-Keynesian recession—had led me to think some other causal forces might be affecting the unemployment rates besides the Keynesian forces of aggregate demand: the forces in Hicks's investment-saving and liquidity preference–money supply (IS-LM) model. Forces appearing in some nonmonetary models, though not in Keynesian models, might be found to shift the "equilibrium unemployment level" (the natural rate of unemployment level)—the level to which the equilibrium path, or "correct-expectations" path, is headed (if no other structural force arose to head it elsewhere).

My first stab at a model was a contribution to the Aalborg conference in honor of Sir John Hicks.[10] The message was that in a two-sector model, the real prices of the capital goods are an additional determinant of the unemployment rate. The mark-up introduced in the paper I wrote with Sid Winter on the customer-market economy for the *Microfoundations* conference was another determinant.

Yet there was a great deal more to be done. I was fortunate to persuade three doctoral candidates and former students of mine at Columbia to help: Hian Teck Hoon to help with modeling beyond the Phelps–Winter model, George T. Kanaginis to do some further modeling, and Gylfi Zoega to help with some substantial statistical testing.[11] Increasingly, we focused on bringing out a monograph synthesizing our work.

In the years from early 1990 to publication in 1994, working with the team in developing nonmonetary models of the employment rate and statistical tests of their implications, I produced a book-length monograph on those implications and the test results. What came out was *Structural Slumps: The Modern Equilibrium Theory of Unemployment, Interest, and Assets*, published by Harvard and much helped by the editor Michael Aronson and a superb copy editor, Kate Schmit.

My enthusiasm over *Structural Slumps* was apparent in the preface condensed and reshaped here:

> [Some] shifts and some long swings in unemployment are . . . not a matter of misperceptions or misforecasts and consequent wage-price misalignments. [Those shifts and swings may be *equilibrium paths* driven by *nonmonetary* mechanisms]: the propensity to quit or shirk, hysteresis effects of idleness, insider-outsider relationships, welfare-state subsidies, rent-seeking unions, balance-sheet factors in financial markets, and the institutional substructure. . . . [E]xisting formulations do not offer a usable intertemporal general-equilibrium theory of these. . . .
>
> This book sets out a [new] paradigm. . . . The equilibrium path [in the sense of a path fulfilling expectations] approaches the natural rate . . . but something has been added: The natural rate moves! . . . [It is] a function of the real structure of the economy. . . . The analytical task has been to [study *how* theoretically the natural rate is driven by elements of the economy's] structure—real sectoral demands, factor supplies, technology, rates of taxation, subsidies, and tariffs.[12]

Theoretical Models

The heart of the theoretical work in *Structural Slumps* presents three complete (though simple) models of the typical developed economy. The first of these models is built around a turnover-training, or incentive-wage, model of the labor market, such as those I began, then recast in "intertemporal terms," and completed with standard treatments of the product market and capital market.[13] In one of the main findings, "the derived demand for labor shifts up not only with increased productivity . . . but with reduced real interest costs as well."[14] Moreover, the explanation continues:

> In what might be called the paradox of demand, . . . increased demand for the output of the consumer good . . . cannot coax firms to employ more; the [resulting] rise of the real interest rate, r, and the associated drop in real asset prices, q, needed to eliminate the excess consumer demand has the perverse side effect of curtailing investment in new employees, thus swelling the equilibrium unemployment rate and ultimately shrinking output and consumption.[15]

Furthermore, a "public debt stimulus"—say a "helicopter-drop of public liability"—making consumers feel wealthier drives up real interest rates and the aggregate rate of unemployment rises. The discussion of this model ends with the caveat that "in the short run, demand-stimulating fiscal policy may lead to expansion of employment and output through the Keynesian channel *before* turning into a net contractionary force via the structural channels explored here."[16]

The second of these general equilibrium models is built around the Phelps–Winter model of the product market, combining it with a version of the Calvo–Bowles shirking model of the labor market and the Blanchard–Yaari model of the capital market, to obtain another general-equilibrium framework.[17] Though it is rather complex, some tools of analysis are obtainable. General-equilibrium output of the consumer good and asset price are determined by supply and demand, so to speak, where the demand-price curve (i.e., the value firms place on their customers *per customer*) intersects the marginal supply–price curve indicating how high the shadow-price of customers must be to elicit a given volume of total output.[18] With this tool, the effects of shocks can be determined. It can be seen that "increased aggregate demand imposes an increased real interest rate . . . through a fall in the real prices of shares. . . . [Further,] the effect of [that] puts the demand price below the supply price (to which it had been equal). On our elasticity condition, this gap can only be closed by a fall of output."[19] The final subsection on this model addressed supply shocks.

The third in this triptych of working models introduces a two-sector fixed-investment model in which production of both the consumer good and the capital good employ labor—producing the consumer good requires capital, whereas producing the capital good does not. This feature is reminiscent of the capital theory introduced around the turn of the century by Böhm-Bawerk, a leader of the Austrian school. (Workers till the grapes and grapes produce the wine.)

After the dynamics of the model were analyzed, using the standard phase diagram, we studied the effects of shocks to this economy—the "Keynesian questions." Supposing that the economy has been in some steady state or steady-growth state, we then explained how, in the event of some fundamental shift, the time-path is changed over the future.

Some early questions related to consumption persisted: What happens in the model if, for example, there is a "helicopter drop" of government bonds, increasing the public debt level, D? The analysis showed that there is an immediate *drop* of the price, q, put on the capital good, which is followed by a declining capital stock, K, and declining q (on top of the immediate drop) as a new rest point is approached asymptotically. The decrease of q in shifting down the derived demand for labor schedule (by more than any forces shifting it up), has a chilling effect on the amount of capital-goods output that firms are willing to supply, which in turn decreases labor demand, thus reducing employment in that sector and the economy-wide wage rate.[20]

Structural Slumps also raised some questions related to investment: What happens if the parameter, λ, measuring the exponential *growth rate* of the current level of labor augmentation parameter, Λ, is suddenly *increased* as a brighter future comes quickly to be incorporated into expectations? The analysis shows that in the present, the price of the capital good, q, abruptly drops at the moment of the increase of λ. "The near-term effect on employment of the drop of q is *contractionary*. . . . [T]he steady-state q is also unambiguously lower, even lower than the post-impact q" since capital, K, cannot keep up with the faster growth of Λ.[21] The West has witnessed over more than four decades the reverse: When Λ slowed to a near stagnation in the 1970s, K easily gained relative to Λ until coming close to capital saturation.

I continued, noting that, in the model under discussion, "an unanticipated increase of [expenditure on consumer goods], in driving up . . . real interest rates, causes the real price of capital goods to jump down, thus making both the natural level of *employment* and the real wage jump down . . . [while] an increased level of public expenditure on the output of the *capital-goods* industry causes the real asset price to jump up and (surprisingly) the real rates of interest to drop, thus making employment and the real wage jump *up*."[22]

In these two examples, Keynesian theory agrees with the structuralist theory only with regard to capital goods expenditure, not consumer good expenditure. In the book I recall that

"Keynes in the early 1930s was an advocate of public works programs as the best or second-best way to pull up employment in the midst of Britain's devastating slump. Later, in the *General Theory* . . . his whole emphasis was on *aggregate demand*."[23] Hayek, on the other hand, argued that increased consumption spending would be contractionary, not expansionary. But he made the mistake of overgeneralizing: appearing to believe that all fiscal stimuli were ineffective.[24] So neither Keynes nor Hayek got it quite right from the perspective of the structuralist theory.

The three modern models I've introduced here, each with a single and distinct asset, are then combined into a *single* model of a multi-asset economy—just like real economies. This synthesis consists of nine variables in nine equations. The right solution—the equilibrium path in which expectations are correct, hence borne out—determines r, u, v, the three qs, and the three state variables (that is the real interest rate, rate of employment, real wage, vector of real asset prices, capital stock, customer stock, and stock of assets). Since this structuralist model has implications, it can be used to make predictions about the consequence of this or that shock or circumstance.

The remaining step was to open the economies of the synthesized model to "international linkages" through investment in fixed capital, investment in customers, and investment in employees. That done, we were ready to estimate the statistical significance and economic importance of the causal variables in our model: the unemployment equation (containing the real interest rate) and the real interest rate equation.

That was the theory. But did this structuralist theory have as much or more power to explain the big downswings and booms as the Keynesian theory? Would this new theory explain as much or more than Keynesian theory explained? The challenge, then, was to "put the new framework to empirical test."[25]

Statistical Findings

Statistical estimation of our econometric model showed "the extent to which the underlying causal [forces in] the structuralist theory do influence the unemployment rates [in] the countries studied."[26] Of central interest, are the implications of this new theory relating to real rates of interest and real prices of assets in open economies—those not so big they have large effects on variables such as the world real interest rate.[27]

With the system of equations in hand, we went to the unemployment equation—more precisely, an equation predicting the unemployment rate over the current year, given the rate in the previous year. Statistical analysis estimated that increases in a nation's public expenditures and tax cuts acted to *decrease* unemployment, while increases in its capital stock and its taxes tended to *increase* unemployment—more or less as the Keynesian theory predicted.[28] (The price of oil was dominant for a time and, after that faded, the public debt was dominant, but, of course, neither one was a Keynesian tool.) Public spending increases and tax cuts were estimated to have the direct effect of *decreasing* the unemployment rate, other things equal—as Keynesianism implied.

But the truth is more complex. Although the *direct* effects of the two Keynesian tools were estimated to decrease the unemployment rate, the same statistical study found *indirect* effects of those two tools on unemployment through the effects on the real rate of interest: A stimulus raises the real rate of interest, which in turn acts to *increase* the unemployment rate. Of course, in a small economy, the real interest rate is largely determined by the prevailing rates in the rest of the world. In an economy large enough that its real interest rate may be increased or decreased, these indirect effects may counterbalance the direct ones or even outweigh them. (Another part of this new theory, developed later, discusses the "behavior of real exchange rates and markups."[29])

As further explained in *Structural Slumps*, "a national increase of public expenditure and of public debt was not found to be expansionary abroad, subject to the same qualification, contrary to the Mundell-Fleming model with flexible exchange rates. Prudence requires putting aside the Keynesian approach for the time being in favor of taking up the structuralist approach."[30] In this more complete analysis, then, the power of the Keynesian tools is significantly weakened—washed away in extreme cases—and the structuralist forces find a place. Our econometric analysis ended on a tone of celebration. "It would be impossible," we wrote, "to look back on the forgoing results without some degree of satisfaction."[31]

These new theoretical findings provide an explanation of macroeconomic developments from the end of the 1950s to the end of the 1980s: "The growth of world public debt, . . . the significant increase in the world level of public expenditure, [and] the [increase in] the world real interest rate. . . . These shocks gave impetus to a major increase of the equilibrium unemployment rate."[32]

MIXED RECEPTION TO THE RESULTS

What was the response to *Structural Slumps*'s theory? Pentti Kouri, a respected Finnish economist, venture capitalist, and art collector—close friend of Mario Draghi, financial partner of George Soros, and admired by all—wrote that the book "is nothing less than a complete reformulation of macroeconomic theory, presenting an alternative to both the New Neoclassical and mainstream Keynesian paradigms."[33] Similarly, Michael Woodford wrote that the book offers "a bold attempt at the synthetic treatment that [recent] work has until now lacked. . . . [T]he new micro-economic models of labor market and product market imperfections are placed at center stage . . . But the book breaks considerable new ground in showing how these various partial analyses can be combined in a single coherent model—and a complete dynamic general equilibrium (ultimately a multi-country model) at that. . . . The project is one of startling ambition, and the book deserves to be widely read and discussed."[34]

In fact, *Structural Slumps* was met not so much with opposition as with resistance. I attended a semiannual research meeting of the National Bureau of Economic Research held in Cambridge, Massachusetts, where the luncheon speaker talked about the recently published *Structural Slumps*. He was quite positive. But in the discussion, a few economists made surprisingly skeptical, if not hostile, comments. Finally, the speaker replied, "C'mon, guys! What do you want?" He put them to shame. The incident speaks of a reluctance to consider the new.

The book did go on to receive some attention by those working in macroeconomics, thanks in part to the review by Michael Woodford. The book also drew positive comments from the *New York Times* and the *Economist*.[35] However, economic policymakers—busy with gathering and analyzing data—did not take into account the structural forces shifting the unemployment path that were brought to light in *Structural Slumps*—or even the Phelps–Friedman concept of a natural (or equilibrium) unemployment rate.

If *Structural Unemployment* was never fully incorporated into standard thinking, the explanation may be in part that some of the theory's drivers lost their fuel. World real interest rates, for example, did not remain high—relative to rates in the 1960s and

1970s—beyond the 1980s. (They reached their plateau in the 1980s, and then returned to the low levels of the 1960s or lower.) For that reason, economists may have lost interest in the real interest rate. The research might also have caused more attention if the main drivers of a nation's growth rate—the growth rate of TFP, usually denoted λ, had been included in the analysis. Yet, the reason for much of the inattention to the results in *Structural Slumps* may be that the economics profession as a whole is reluctant to pay the cost of mastering and incorporating new findings.

Looking back, I felt fortunate to have provided first a microeconomic foundation for the Keynesian model of unemployment with the introduction of wage and price expectations (leading to the natural unemployment rate), and next a nonmonetary (i.e., structural) foundation for a far broader model of the path of unemployment: a model of the forces affecting the natural rate. These steps, although important, could not reasonably be viewed in my mind as radical steps in economic theory.

I would also say that these advances—the idea that firms hit by a downturn in deciding their own wage rates form expectations of the rate of change of others' wage rates and the idea of structural shifts in the natural rate—had showed some creativity but were not deeply imaginative. Most economists encountering Keynes's stickiness, or wondering whether the natural rate does not shift, would have come up with something like my micromacro hypothesis sooner or later. (Economists then were not comfortable with the conception of humans possessing autonomy, or agency.)

In the remaining half of the 1990s I wondered whether I might be fortunate enough to break into a subject that was radically different from past work and would require a deeper creativity than I had drawn on before. While thinking about that, I took some time out to write a short work.

REWARDING WORK: ADDING TO RAWLS

The frustration in the 1950s and 1960s with the obstacles to American women having careers—expressed by Betty Friedan's *The Feminine Mystique* in 1963—did finally result in women entering the labor force and climbing some steps up the ladder. The resentment felt by Black people in the United States leading to riots in the mid- to late 1960s—attributed to white racism in the 1968 Kerner Report—did finally result in appreciable numbers of Black people holding higher positions and entering industries and professions not previously open to them. Yet the meager pay of jobholders with serious economic disadvantages remained to be fully addressed.

In the mid-1990s, with *Structural Slumps* behind me, these concerns led me to start thinking about what the government could do to pull up those wages net of tax at the bottom. I recall going up the Hudson to present my thoughts at a conference at Bard College in Annandale-on-Hudson around 1990. There was great interest in what could be done to raise very low wages. It is true that the U.S. Earned Income Tax Credit (EITC), championed by Senator Russell Long (D–LA) and signed into law in 1975, served to pull up the bottom after-tax wage rates—and a very elegant instrument it was. It also widened the opportunity of some working-age people to opt for employment rather than to remain self-employed. But the EITC did not go far enough to ensure a decent living for the less advantaged.

I noticed that the discussion was solely on the pay and not at all on the work itself. Public policy ought to address the importance of work itself as well as the wages paid. Society will not fare well if a great many working-age people are unaware of the nonpecuniary rewards that work in a healthy economy provides. So economic policy must ensure that wage rates offered to the lower echelons of society are at least high enough to draw them into the experience of work as well as to supply income.

My book, *Rewarding Work: How to Restore Participation and Self-Support to Free Enterprise*, published by Harvard in 1997, introduced two ideas into the discussion of wages and work.

The first idea is the value of self-support. People draw satisfactions from being self-supporting and from being a provider to others in need—one's child or an elderly parent or other to whom one is obligated. I wrote, "The material rewards from work become of huge importance when they are large enough to enable a person to be self-supporting—to earn by one's own efforts the opportunity to enjoy the basic comforts, to have a family, and to share to a degree in the life of the community. Few circumstances undermine a person's self-esteem more than the dependency on others for such material support."[36] Charles Dickens, for example, was haunted all his life by the inability of his father to get by, sporadically depending on his son for support.

The second idea is the value of participating (as one chooses) in the work going on in society's economy. Measures to pull working-age people from money-making activities outside the economy into the economy's jobs enable these people to find deep rewards—the rewards of work esteemed by Thorsten Veblen, William James, Alfred Marshall, and William Julius Wilson. (Later I saw that both Søren Kierkegaard and Friedrich Nietzsche were influential forerunners.) From this perspective, government measures to raise wage rates from meager levels to levels offering such rewards would be a profound act. As I wrote,

> The disadvantaged workers' prospects of self-realization and social participation—not just income or even [wage] earnings—matter enormously, and these prospects may be very poor no matter

how reliably the safety net of the welfare system or the family averts material poverty. To have those deeply desired things requires having a productive and visible place in society, hence, for most people, [a place] in the market economy—not work in the underworld or domestic work concealed from view in someone's home. . . . [M]any disadvantaged workers may have only a fragile or sporadic orientation toward jobholding. . . . Their performance as employees suffers, which in turn reduces the wages that employers can afford to pay such workers, which causes a further fall of wages and a rise of unemployment as well.[37]

The concern expressed in *Rewarding Work* is not inequality in general—not even the inequality between the income of the median earner and the highest earners, which now appears to be drawing more ire than the inequality between workers around the bottom and those around the middle. I summed up the problem as follows:

The pay of America's lowest lifetime earners has become so remote from the pay of the *median* earner as to make them a class apart. . . . The gap in pay casts a pall over poor communities and leaves a legacy of disadvantage for the next generation. . . .

This devaluation of work imposes costs throughout society. . . . [M]en [are] led away from work into drugs and crime. . . . The price of policies to mollify the working class is far more costly . . . than a policy going to the root of the problem . . . to raise the wage of less-paid work.[38]

How was this to be done? To achieve this, the book calls for an *employment subsidy* and works out an example with which to calculate the cost of a hypothetical subsidy. The social benefits, however, go beyond gains made by the low earners. The epilogue comments, "By empowering those with a relatively low earning power to be self-supporting . . . and by drawing into the capitalist mainstream millions of less productive persons who are now depending on welfare, workfare, begging, hustling, and crime, the employment subsidy plan would improve the quality of life for everyone else."[39]

Over the late 1990s, there was a flurry of discussions and conferences in academia on employment subsidies. At the time, many governments around the world were discussing poverty. The Singapore government, when the redoubtable Lee Kuan Yew was still governor, instituted a program of wage subsidies stemming in significant part from the proposal in my book— thanks in large measure to the contribution, including technical input, of my former student and frequent coauthor, Hian Teck Hoon. In the summer of 1997 and 1998, when visiting Jean-Paul Fitoussi in Paris at the French Economic Observatory, I learned that the French government took some measures in the same spirit. So many other measures were taken, however, that one could hardly view France as having adopted a full-scale program of low-wage subsidies.

Around this time, interest in employment subsidies grew among many including those within the offices of the OECD in Paris. A conference of delegates from member nations was held in 2001, and I was appointed to make the opening address in which to make the argument for employment subsidies in the member countries. I was excited to see the British delegation was keenly in favor of employment subsidies. My hopes that the Clinton administration would support an employment subsidy plan were dashed when the U.S. delegation spoke. They expressed concern that legislation of such a plan would put at risk the EITC on which many women with young children were dependent.

I was disappointed, of course, and did not think well of the Clinton administration on this count, notwithstanding Bill Clinton's brilliance (in a couple of meetings with him in the next two decades, I was quite impressed by his knowledge). Indeed, I was disappointed at the rejection of the employment subsidies idea by the great majority of economists in the West. It seems that the prevailing attitude in the population did not encourage politicians to launch any new initiative.

The social cost of this inaction was considerable. Not only did wages at the low end receive no lift from governments in the United States and most other Western nations, but those wages steadily fell relative to national income—as they had been doing since the early 1970s—right up to the start of the COVID-19 pandemic.

Soon after *Rewarding Work* was published, I telephoned Jack Rawls to tell him that I hadn't felt I could base the argument on economic justice, which he had done. Before I could go on to convey the arguments I had used, he exclaimed that "You can't!" adding, "Not in this climate." His understanding was an immense relief. I was also consoled by the fact that I had linked to Rawls the concept of a surplus from cooperation—"a gain from the cooperation of different kinds of workers. How these gains are in fact distributed depends on prevailing taxes, subsidies, and so forth."[40]

Rewarding Work also had some intellectual success. It earned the attention of some of the leading economists and other thought leaders in the United States. One day, Samuelson— by this time, well into his nineties and working at home—and I got to talking over the phone. *Rewarding Work* came up, and he told me that he kept it sticking out from his bookcase "so it would be easy to find."

A subsequent conference held at the Russell Sage Foundation in 2003—a gathering of a galaxy of leaders in the field, including James Heckman, Hian Teck Hoon, Dale Mortensen, Christopher Pissarides, Dennis Snower, and others—introduced another dimension not explicit in *Rewarding Work*'s case for employment subsidies to the low-paid: inclusion. As noted in my introduction to the conference volume *Designing Inclusion*, the widening deficiency of inclusion over the late 1970s and 1980s resulted in a marginalization of the less qualified workers: participation of men in the labor force had fallen more, and their unemployment had risen more.[41]

To some commentators, it was noted, deficient inclusion is "nothing more than an instance of *income inequality*."[42] But this deficiency of inclusion has societal effects beyond those of income inequality, wage inequality, and inequality in general. Having a job and earning enough in that job to be independent are crucial in their own right. Failure to achieve these objectives is apt to deprive a person of gains in knowledge, information, achievements, personal growth, and self-esteem that would have otherwise been acquired. And when a community is dominated by these problems, the effects extend to drug trade and the loss of public safety. "Yet," as Derek Bok once said, "we continue to talk . . . as if income statistics captured the phenomenon in some meaningful way."[43]

Looking back at the poor economic experience in the Western nations, it is striking that their governments have failed not only to adequately address the meager rewards of the less advantaged working in the economy, but they have also failed to address the severe loss of economic growth. As a result of that slowdown of growth, at least in part, participation rates among men continue to decline and participation rates among women have stopped rising. In fact, many governments in Western Europe had blundered in bypassing private capital and crimping its prerogatives: making layoffs difficult, propping up inefficient firms, expanding public sector jobs, and interfering with decisions better made by private business. This is a key feature of corporatism—the doctrine that corporations and most other private entities are best put under government control. Many governments in Europe and the United States, too, drew back from intervening with employment subsidies, hiring subsidies, and similarly intended initiatives that would channel some of the power of the market to regain inclusion.

The required policy, I argued in a 1997 paper, was the reverse: The Continent needed to liberate its enterprises. As I wrote then, however, "Free enterprise alone will [not] shrink unemployment on the Continent to the levels of the early '70s . . . nor will it deliver in 'Anglo-Saxon countries' the lift to low-end pay and low-end jobs needed so badly there. Another reform is needed: intervention to redirect market forces toward integrating low-end workers."[44] The West, I concluded then, "can refit competitive capitalism for renewed pursuit of growth and the broadest opportunity, thus renewing the Enlightenment vision of what the West might be."[45]

Was that enough? Although that initiative was necessary, I was beginning to doubt that it would be or could be sufficient. Some years into the next decade, I began to sense that roots of growth, and job satisfaction too, lay deeper.

7

A *FESTSCHRIFT*, A NOBEL,
AND A NEW HORIZON

The 2000s began auspiciously. In New York City, the Metropolitan Opera celebrated the new century with a gala of performances and dinner marking the arrival of 2000, and then celebrated the new century again with a gala marking the arrival of 2001. After dinner that night, René Pape, the world's greatest basso in Germanic roles, gave a thrilling rendition of some of the great Cole Porter songs. When he finished, Maestro James Levine leapt to his feet, as did all of us. What an artist! Later, when Viviana and I ventured onto the dance floor, there was Pape dancing with his wife. What an evening! It was natural to wonder whether things might go on that way over the years ahead.

Certainly, the economy in 2001 was looking up in important ways. Unemployment had been trending down for two decades after fluctuations at high levels, and Britain, along with parts of the Continent, was steadily gaining after more than two difficult decades. Growth in the U.S. economy, as measured by the growth rate of total factor productivity (TFP), had picked up over the second half of the 1990s, so there was hope that growth would remain more rapid than it had been following the onset of semistagnation in the early 1970s—that, somehow, Silicon

Valley would continue to be humming with new products and methods. I recall in those years a late dinner with friends in lower Manhattan at a restaurant alive with the energy of young people, many of them no doubt making fortunes.

Yet not everything was coming up roses. Trade was cutting both ways. The expansion of international trade that came with the stunning economic development of Asian economies in general, and with South Korea and China in particular, brought important gains from trade—including a lift to the profit rates of some big exporting firms in the West—but were a drag on wages and employment in parts of U.S. industry. (The theoretical possibility of that is shown in my textbook *Political Economy*.) Recent years also saw a serious drop in male labor force participation. Moreover, the downward slide of job satisfaction continued and the near stagnation of wages in the whole "bottom half" was unceasing.

In that year, Roman Frydman pointed out to me that with my seventieth birthday coming up in a few years it was not too soon to begin the organization of the traditional *Festschrift* in my honor. Roman recruited Philippe Aghion, Joseph Stiglitz, and Michael Woodford to join him in finding the speakers for the conference and writing the introduction to the conference volume that followed.

CELEBRATING MY PROJECT

I knew little about what was planned. I learned the conference was carved into four parts over two days and each part was to be followed by remarks by some *emimence gris*: the leading Keynesian James Tobin, the leading neoclassical Robert Lucas, and the leading growth modeler Robert Solow. It was expected that Robert Merton and John Rawls would also join. Yet I had a feeling that someone was missing—Paul Samuelson, the god that I had worshiped from the time I read his textbook in 1952. Philippe leapt into action, and within a couple of days, he told me that Paul would be there and would be the keynote speaker. That was enormously gratifying.

Then something terrible happened. On September 11, two planes crashed into the twin towers of the World Trade Center in lower Manhattan. I will never forget starting out the door early that morning when Viviana told me there was enormous smoke coming out of one of the twin towers—an icon of the city dear to all New Yorkers. This was awful and traumatic— the huge loss of life and the depressing loss of morale in the city and the whole nation. It was also scary, as security concerns led to closing all the city's commercial airports. Travel to New York was blocked. Ultimately, the attacks on the Trade Center and the Pentagon led to instituting domestic safeguards against terrorism, the ugly rise of discrimination toward Muslims in the United States, and a new phase in foreign policy toward Afghanistan and the Middle East.

A week or so after the attack, I went to see Jonathan Cole, Columbia's provost, who had helped clear the way for the big conference. Ought I cancel the conference coming up in October, or stick to the plan even though many, even most, conferees may be unwilling or unable to travel to the event? Jonathan, fearing it might not be possible to get the conference going another time, urged me to stick to the plan, which I did. Then, one day Viviana and I saw a commercial aircraft heading along the Hudson River for LaGuardia Airport. New York was an open city again. The conference was held as planned and fortunately, very few absences resulted from the horror of September 11.

In the large conference room, well over a hundred participants filled the room and there was Paul, standing near the front. After I expressed to him my thanks, we chatted for a moment. "You know," he said, "Schumpeter was not an Austrian"—meaning not that he hadn't been in Graz but that he hadn't been a member of the Austrian school. "Yes," I said, "I know." (Paul's thought, I supposed, was that Schumpeter's thinking, which Paul knew well, was totally neoclassical, while the Austrian school was not markedly neoclassical in their theorizing. Later, I was to emphasize that the fault in Schumpeter's theory of innovation was precisely its neoclassicism.) Then suddenly Paul was called to the dais. Samuelson's speech began with my education in economics and went on to cite virtually all of my first decade of theoretical work. He continued at his most lyrical:

> You might say this was Picasso's classical period. I knew of his innovations well and not only because Solow and I were pedaling in the same bicycle marathon. Often I was a free-rider boosted ahead by Ned's free efforts . . . Phelps establishes his credentials in the easy micro and macro of Hicks-Danzig-Debreu: Santa Claus domains of convex sets and the differentiable calculus of variations. [But] would he advance into the unpromising lands of increasing returns to scale, asymmetric information, lumpiness, and all those other imperfections undreamed of in the philosophies of the equilibrium mongers?
>
> The answer is a resounding, Yes. To sum up my hagiographic panegyric, I shall steal a few lines from Phillipe Aghion, who "sees Phelps's contribution as basically *one* project: *to introduce imperfect information and knowledge, imperfect competition, and market frictions* into macroeconomics"—and, I would add, into microeconomics as well. To polish Max Planck's dictum: Science does

progress funeral by funeral—as the chorus of Phelpses and Stiglitzes explicates those many ways that palsy can afflict the invisible hand of Smith, Say, and Lucas.[1]

Bob Mundell commented to me in the break that Paul had an extraordinary ability to generate excitement at a conference. I ought to have added that he did more than that: Paul openly credited me in public for having taken the lead in introducing *imperfect information* and *imperfect knowledge* into macroeconomics. I could not have asked for more.

The conference was far more impressive than I had imagined. On the first day, papers were given by Michael Woodford, Gregory Mankiw, Guillermo Calvo, and then by Bruce Greenwald and Joseph Stiglitz—followed by general comments by Robert Lucas. These presentations were followed by papers from Roman Frydman, Mordechai Kurz, and David Laibson, which were followed by Robert Pollak's general comments. On the second day, Dale Mortensen gave the first paper, followed by Christopher Pissarides, James Heckman, Philippe Aghion, Daron Acemoglu, Charles Jones, and Jess Benhabib. (Robert Solow gave general comments that are contained in the *Festschrift* volume, but time constraints prevented his reading them.)

Yet more did come. In the introduction to the conference volume *Knowledge, Information, and Expectations in Modern Economics: In Honor of Edmund S. Phelps* published by Princeton in 2003, Roman and his coorganizers, Philippe, Joe, and Michael, wrote of "the 'Phelps Program' in Macroeconomics"—referring to my work on unemployment and labor force participation in the nearly three decades from "Phillips Curves" to *Structural Slumps*. The introduction noted, as Samuelson had paraphrased, that my main contribution was "introducing imperfect information, with its associated frictions, and imperfect knowledge, with its consequent complications, into macroeconomics."[2] I am grateful to them for producing such an excellent and supportive introduction to such an impressive conference volume. I have always been grateful to Roman for conceiving the magnificent conference and resulting conference volume and grateful to all of them for their superb work in contributing hugely to the end results.

What of the conference following Paul's exciting speech? The event was impressive and still remembered by participants, some of whom recalled it decades later, even though it did not run perfectly. Rawls—sad to say—was unable to travel, and both Jim Tobin and Bob Merton were unexpectedly hospitalized. (Bill Brainard, a Cowles Foundation colleague, read some notes he had prepared with Jim.)

After all the Friday papers and commentaries had been given, I went to the front of the room to explain the dinner arrangements. But before I could speak, Bob Mundell, who was seated front-row center, began applauding and then every one of the 120 attendees jumped to their feet and applauded. No moment in my career was more moving.

That day was a tough act to follow. The second day, however, featured rich contributions in the morning on the "real" (i.e., nonmonetary) determinants of unemployment—that is, the "equilibrium" determinants, roughly speaking. Yet they did well in addressing and extending my work in the 1990s on modeling the market forces bringing the unemployment rate toward its "equilibrium path"—equilibrium in the sense of development in keeping with expectations.

This wondrous *Festschrift*—the conference and the conference volume—turned out to be a watershed in my career, although that was not foreseeable at the time. It marked the end to my work in the four fields of macroeconomics carved out by the organizers. I was far, though, from leaving the field of economic theory.

A NEW HORIZON

In the months that followed, I began to think about leaving what had been my primary interests—unemployment theory started by Keynes, national saving theory started by Frank Ramsey, and economic justice started by Rawls—and trying to start a *new* theory—a departure with some fundamental consequences. I needed to get away from their shadows. Even in an earlier essay, "A Life in Economics," I had noticed that "there is a big difference between scanning existing models for their unnoticed implications . . . and acquiring an independent empirical sense of how in some overlooked or misunderstood way the economy works."[3] (Of course, economies may differ in the "way" they "work.")

The way forward, undoubtedly, was not just a matter of taking the "road less traveled," but rather taking a road that looked like it might be going in a desirable direction. What was needed was, yes, creativity, but the creativity to form a new vision—or intuition—of what drives the economy forward. This seems to me to be on a different level from conceiving hypotheses as to why money wage rates are sticky, as Keynes observed, or how much of the swings in unemployment are the effect of shifts in the Keynes–Hicks IS-LM model and how much by shifts in the structural forces brought up by Knight and Hayek.

As it happened, I began around this time to look into "economic growth"—sustained growth of TFP, to be more precise. I wondered, might the accepted thinking on the source of growth—the road widely followed—be so narrow as to fall seriously short? Might there be at times in some parts of the world deep sources of innovation—sources quite different from the exogenous shocks and parameter shifts introduced into neoclassical growth models, both deterministic and stochastic? Could it be that in many a nation most of its sources lie in the people, and hence what kind of people they are? What drives the innovation that is indigenous to a nation? I had just turned sixty-eight, and I was fortunate to have the next two decades in which to explore these ideas. I could hardly wait. There was no looking back. I was looking for a new start.

Pieces of the puzzle came slowly. In the months that followed, I sometimes came across uses of the term "flourishing." Its meaning was alluded to by Tom Nagel in his discussion of personal growth, which, I thought, captured quite well the non-pecuniary rewards of involvement in innovating.[4]

In early 2003, first in January at the annual Shaw Foundation Lecture at Singapore Management University, and then in March at the Royal Institute of Economic Affairs at Chatham House, I gave a lecture on the innovation stemming from within a nation—indigenous innovation. It started in the right direction: "A high-performing economy enables its participants to go beyond living long and keeping healthy and secure to engaging in careers offering problem-solving and personal growth. The best performers tend to have it all: [the highest] productivity, [the most] rewarding work and [widest] inclusion. . . . This suggests that some countries have acquired some *elixir* boosting performance that is absent in the others, putting them at risk of bad performance in all or most respects. My thesis is that the property I call *dynamism* is that force."[5] This was the first time that I used the term "dynamism" and the first allusion to powers to create.

Later in the lecture, I put together some early thoughts on the sources of this "dynamism." This was a slow slog and proceeded one step at a time: "For an economy to present opportunities for mental challenge and personal growth . . . [t]here have to be new ideas for ways to produce goods or for new goods to produce so that there will be new problems to be solved and new capabilities attained. [Society] . . . wants purposeful change that aims for productivity benefits exceeding the costs. So . . . there have to be institutions that permit and foster a high degree of dynamism, where we can think of dynamism as the normal, or average, flow of well-directed innovation."[6]

I went on to point out that this "dynamism theory" of a nation's innovation differs radically from the "entrepreneur theory" expounded by Schumpeter in the 1911 book that made him famous, *Theorie der wirthschaftlichen Entwicklung* (the English translation, *Theory of Economic Development*, came out in 1934). His theory centers on the "art" of the "entrepreneur" in noticing and evaluating the commercial value of the scientific discoveries that Arthur Spiethoff (a contemporary of Schumpeter) wrote of and on the daring of the entrepreneur to introduce into markets some applications of these discoveries.[7] With the interest in economic growth after World War II, Robert Solow was inspired to publish in 1956 a model of productivity growth driven by exogenous "technical progress" in the spirit of Schumpeter's theory.[8]

In contrast, the "dynamism" I introduced in my 2003 lecture referred to actions taken *within* a nation that generate innovating. This reference was to what I would later term *indigenous* innovation—innovation springing from inside the nation, in particular from ordinary people working in its economy—*not* the innovation sparked by the discoveries of "scientists and navigators," which Spiethoff celebrated, and their frequently daring commercial applications by "entrepreneurs," which Schumpeter celebrated.

The remainder of that lecture focused solely on the theme that "some institutions are vital for dynamism." No doubt, innovation is bound to be crimped or infeasible if the needed institutions function poorly or some institutions are missing. But an adequate theory of dynamism—of what fuels it and sparks it—what it derives from, in other words—does not stop there.

What was missing in this lecture was a theory, let alone substantial evidence, of the forces—the root sources—driving, or fueling, this "dynamism." It is true that humankind is born with the creativity needed to enable, or fuel, the conception, or development, of new products and methods. But what is it that sparks the indigenous innovation in a nation? A link was missing between the possession of creativity and the eagerness to use it to imagine—to conceive and achieve the development of new things.

I took a step forward in the 2005 manuscript, "The Economic Performance of Nations," turning to another, perhaps more fundamental level, although institutions remained in the background: "We cannot have a reasoned discussion of [economic] performance of institutions," I wrote, "until we are willing and able to specify the kind of economy we want to have . . . what a desirable business life is. . . . High productivity is just one element of good economic performance."[9] I continued: "Enlisting the minds of the jobholders [and] offering challenge in problem solving leads people to discover some of their talents and causes them to expand their abilities. The personal growth that comes from the discovery, development [, and use] of talents is basic to what is often called job satisfaction."[10]

Is this conception of high performance generally accepted? In Europe? Anywhere? The notion of high economic performance, of the desirable economy that I have just outlined, is often said to be peculiar to the United States. Probably many readers will feel that this notion of performance—more broadly, the elevation of work and business—does resonate in varying degrees and respects with some memorable American writers, among them Benjamin Franklin, Ralph Waldo Emerson, Abraham Lincoln,

William James, John Dewey, John Rawls, Richard Rorty, and Derek Curtis Bok. However, the commonly held impression that this conception of high performance is foreign to European values is unfounded. The origins of some of these desires go back some centuries and raise issues that have long been argued. The humanist thesis that discovery, independence, enterprise, and participation are the route to personal development and achievement was, after all, first articulated and developed by Europeans. This humanism grew out of ancient Greece, the Renaissance, and the Enlightenment.[11]

Yet this discussion, while adding to the Singapore-Chatham House lecture, did not appear to reach what felt like a logically complete and sufficiently clear theory of the *non-Schumpeterian innovation* that I had in mind and vaguely hinted at.

In May 2006, I had another at-bat at the Conference on Entrepreneurship and Economic Growth, held in Tegernsee on the outskirts of Munich and organized by the Max Planck Institute and the Kauffman Foundation. I presented my paper entitled "Toward a Model of Innovation and Performance Along the Lines of Knight, Keynes, Hayek and M. Polanyi."

Addressing an audience of mostly Europeans, I began with a critique of the theory of innovation founded and developed by the German Historical School, which then led me to the theory I was in the process of developing. In the first part of this three-part paper, I gave my respects to the early attention paid to innovation by the leaders of the German Historical School, the German Spiethoff in the early 1900s and later the Swede Gustav Cassell and the Austrian Schumpeter:

> Thanks to them, economic advances became a leading object of research for decades to come. Their work linked innovations to forces taken to be *exogenous* to the market economy, such as

technological breakthroughs and the opening up of overseas markets and materials. A new discovery created new outlets for investment. The investments made "express the zeal of employers to profit by meeting the increased demand of the community for fixed capital," Cassel wrote in his *Theory of the Social Economy* (1923). This provided a useful view of some *historically* important innovations . . . sparked by . . . shocks *outside* [the economy].[12]

From this perspective, Schumpeter's role was to make this very neoclassical theory significantly richer and more realistic: "Schumpeter . . . extended this neoclassical theory . . . [in adding that these] innovations required an 'entrepreneur' with the 'will' to undertake the venture—generally in 'new firms.' . . . In this system, bankers selected the investment projects to back. Finally, the successful start-ups stimulated other entrepreneurs to imitate and together they caused 'creative destruction' of some existing products and jobs in the process of creating new ones."[13] Schumpeter's success surely owed something to his effective writing. (At Amherst's Merrill Center for Economics, I heard his translator, British economist Redvers Opie, say that Schumpeter studied closely the translation, chapter by chapter. A student of mine fluent in German couldn't find in it any deviation from the original.)

But, in what had come to be my view of the matter, innovativeness in a nation—a big nation, at any rate—comes largely from the realizations of new ideas springing from *within* the business sector of the nation's economy. My paper states: "Capitalist systems are private-ownership systems distinguished by openness to implementing *new commercial ideas*—ideas for new products and methods—and by decentralized, pluralistic mechanisms for *selecting* the ideas to finance and providing the needed capital and incentives."

Although Schumpeter introduced the concept of what is often called the Schumpeterian entrepreneur, who launches commercial products made feasible by the shock of a discovery somewhere in the world, he had no sense of what started coming up as he was putting his pen down, including Henri Bergson's "creative evolution" (1912), Knight's "uncertainty" (1921), and Keynes's "probability" (1921)—the latter two publications having been delayed by World War I. Schumpeter had not broken away from neoclassical or premodern thinking.

I went on to write: "The mechanisms of this model . . . are strikingly pre-modern. . . . Schumpeter's very concept of an innovation is different from that of the theorists of the interwar period. . . . The Schumpeterian entrepreneur seems to be a vessel for acting on information about unexploited opportunities detected and talked about by members of the business community."[14]

The second part of the paper for the Max Plank conference moves on from characterizing and critiquing Schumpeter's neoclassical approach to "sketch the core element of a model capturing the essential aspects of a capitalist economy in the sense of an economy driven by proposals of private business participants to private financiers for backing of innovative projects."[15]

The first objective was to picture a micro-based mechanism governing what could be called the "flow-supply" of new ideas to the innovation market coming from entrepreneurs and the "flow-demand" for new ideas coming from financiers. This sketch went on to consider how certain market forces, such as the circumstances and expectations of entrepreneurs and those financing them, affect the outcome of their interaction. Since innovative ideas were central to the performance of businesses, it was important, I felt, to have models of the supply of entrepreneurial ideas to the market and the demand for them by managers and financiers.[16]

Lest this image of the economy seemed awfully unreal, I pointed to visible evidence of such interactions. I had supposed for simplicity that, periodically, all of the entrepreneurs who have hit upon a new idea travel to a sort of "fair" to seek financing of its development and marketing. A larger number of financiers attend the fair to seek entrepreneurial projects to invest in or lend to—like today's hedge funds and venture capitalists. (I was delighted to learn about a year ago that such fairs actually take place.[17] I mentioned this image of a fair to Richard Robb, who was teaching advanced students and running a hedge fund and writing a book—"like Keynes," I like to say about him. He said he had recently gone to just such a fair. I asked him whether there was a clockwise motion. He said there was.)

This crude model was nothing like the Yale model of the capital market devised by Irving Fisher and James Tobin. That model implicitly supposes there is *no ambiguity* about the promise of each proposed project, so there is agreement among the financiers about the value of each project. But, in general, the arrival of someone with a new idea for something creates ambiguity about exactly what the new thing is and hence what, roughly, the demand for it would be.[18]

In the third part of this paper, I address the role of innovative opportunity in economic performance. After introducing the supply of new entrepreneurial ideas springing up from the economy and the demand for *new ideas* from entrepreneurs capable of providing *development* of their ideas (and a pluralism of financiers with a background sufficient to make a *good selection* of these ideas and entrepreneurs for backing)—all of which is central to innovation and thus to high economic performance— the paper speaks of the "capabilities" of the participants required for the creation of new ideas.[19] It is clear that I understood little about the "sources of those capabilities."

I did sense, however, the importance of people's possession of these capabilities and, no doubt, the importance of people's desire to express those capabilities—thus the importance of personal growth and having an economy that provides people with prospects of careers generating mental stimulation, intellectual challenge, opportunities for problem-solving, and the chance to exercise creativity and to feel pride in earning one's way. I understood that this was the philosophy of life that runs from Aristotle to Cervantes to William James and Henri Bergson.[20]

I went on to express a thought I came to see as unclear—one that started with the Singapore-Chatham House lecture:

> If an economy's capability in providing rewarding work is to go from some barely adequate level to a level out of which can come substantial personal development, the *economy* needs the *dynamism* to generate a sufficient flow of innovation. . . . *Capitalism's* dynamism—the abundance of the entrepreneurial ideas it stimulates, the diligence with which entrepreneurs are motivated to develop their idea, and the acumen of a pluralism of financiers in selecting the ideas for backing—generates successive entrepreneurial *ideas* that serve to provide mental stimulation in the workplace, to pose new problems to be solved, and thus to open the way to self-realization and gratification.[21]

This thesis would have been better expressed if it had made explicit that "dynamism"—where it is found—derives from the *people*, not from the incentives that capitalism or any other economic system presents—although incentives are necessary if people are to exercise their creativity in desirable directions.

For there to be wide indigenous innovation in a country, it is crucial that the *people* have the *qualities* needed for dynamism. It remains true, of course, that poor organization of a capitalist economy can block any expression of the people's dynamism—whatever innovations it is able to generate through other sources (such as a science foundation or adopting new advances in other countries).

I was to improve on the thoughts expressed in this essay over the next several years. Despite some limitations and missteps, these thoughts were going in the right direction. The main subject of this paper was the creativity found in humankind and the rewards that come from exercising it as well as the benefits these rewards bring to society.

THE NOBEL PRIZE

In the 2000s, the subject of a Nobel Prize began to come to mind from time to time—mine and that of a few friends. With Bob Mundell having won it for creating international macroeconomics in 1999, Amartya Sen for his contribution to welfare economics in 1998, and Robert Lucas for a neoclassical macroeconomics in 1995, I had a feeling that my time had come. This feeling was heightened by the large and cosmopolitan group that joined the celebration in 2001. There was a sense that the enthusiasm shown at the *Festschrift* would be conveyed to members of the Nobel Prize Committee. When that didn't work, I was told that a band of supporters organized a wheelbarrow full of nominations that was delivered to the Committee, but the organizers were told that was not productive—indeed, counterproductive. Yet I had my work to think about. I had learned not to have expectations of a Nobel Prize.

On Monday, October 9, 2006, the call came. Many people have asked me what that experience was like. I was put through to Gunnar Öquist, permanent secretary of the Swedish Royal Academy of Sciences, to hear from him the news of the Nobel Prize. Thinking that I might have missed something, I asked him whether I would be sharing the prize. "No," he replied, "you are the sole recipient." Viviana and I were overjoyed. So would my parents have been, had they lived to that time.

One of the few callers to reach me that morning was Paul Samuelson. With great energy, he said, "You won it, and you won it alone." There were higher awards and some marvelous celebrations to come, but I didn't need more than that phone call from Öquist and that minute or two with Samuelson. Columbia organized a press conference introduced by President Lee Bollinger and featuring an engaging recollection by Jeffrey Sachs, who recalled the excitement over the arrival at the Harvard Book Store of copies of *Microeconomic Foundations*. Charlotte Morgan told me that someone from the *Charlie Rose Show* called to invite me on the show but couldn't get through that night.

Among the many memorable events during Nobel Week in Stockholm, a few moments have stayed with me. On the first evening, a small dinner at which the awardee and the Nobel Prize Committee have an opportunity to meet was held in the Red Room, where a century ago writer and artist August Strindberg led the movement to bring Sweden into the modern world. The choice of that room gave me a sense of the importance that the country attached to the Nobel Prize.

The Swedes were wonderfully kind. At the grand banquet, Viviana was seated next to the newly elected prime minister. We were given a long limousine and the best guides. Hans Tson Söderström and his wife invited us to dinner. Another day, we were shown a room full of Assar Lindbeck's paintings. The whole week was quite special and memorable. One day following a luncheon, we were driven through heavy traffic to a classroom where, to my surprise, Peter Howitt was at the blackboard lecturing the students about my 1968 *Journal of Political Economy* paper on the place of expectations in wage-setting—and making it ever-so-clear and effortless. I felt grateful to Peter for that.

After a hugely admiring presentation of my work at the press conference held by a member of the Nobel Prize Committee, Lars Calmfors, a reporter piped up, "Why did it take you so long then [to receive the award]?" It had been hard for me to understand. But they had to be especially cautious about conferring a prize to just one person. Recently, it dawned on me that after my award, hardly anyone has been a sole recipient. It could not have been easy for them to grant that distinction to me.

At the conclusion of Nobel Week, the awardees met at the Foundation to receive the Nobel Medal and say goodbye to our hosts. I approached Gunnar Öquist, and as we shook hands, he said to me in that deep voice of his, "Use it well."[22]

After Stockholm and a good rest over the holidays, there were more awards, some quite wonderful. One touching award was the 2008 *Premio Pico della Mirandola*, given to me, Mario Draghi, and (posthumously) Luciano Pavarotti (his wife accepted his gold statue). It was also delightful to have the Medal of the Chevalier of the Legion d'Honneur bestowed on me by Christine Lagarde and to mingle with friends over champagne and hors d'oeuvres on a sunny Paris day in June 2009. Later, I was awed in 2012 to be named Honorary Patron, University Philosophical Society, Trinity College, Dublin, just after Nancy Pelosi and decades after Winston Churchill.

These occasions were all hugely enjoyable and broadening. But other things were important too, among them the development and direction of a new research center at Columbia, the Center on Capitalism and Society—and the teaching, which had not gone away.

The Center had grown out of conversations that Roman Frydman, Andrzej Rapaczynski, and I had over the year I was in London at the European Bank for Reconstruction and Development. Roman recalls that when he began to describe the idea of the Center to William McDonough at the Federal Reserve Bank of New York, McDonough jumped straight up from his chair. That was encouraging. When the idea took shape, I brought it to Columbia's provost, Jonathan Cole, and later to the president, George Rupp; and before the academic year was over, the Center was authorized. (Rupp, a theologian specializing in Luther and the Protestant Reformation, seemed unlikely to react badly to carrying out research on capitalism—its credits and debits.)

Early in 2001, the Center had begun to take shape. Pentti Kouri, who had quit Yale but remained a brilliant economist, had the idea of a journal, which he and Roman helped to start up. Richard Robb, who had recently joined the School of International and Public Affairs at Columbia University and Pentti formed the Center's Advisory Board. I became the director and, a few years later, Miranda Featherstone, who had been my secretary, became the administrative manager. We invited Amar Bhide to be the editor of the journal, and he secured funding from Kauffman Foundation to start it with Berkeley Electronic Press. The members who joined me in those first years included Roman Frydman, Andrzej Rapaczynski, Amar Bhide, Richard Nelson, Glenn Hubbard, Joseph Stiglitz, Bruce Greenwald, Merritt Fox, and Pentti Kouri.

My first responsibility as the director was to find the space and funds as well as to give direction to the Center's activities— its conferences, publications, and research projects. In January 2002, I invited Jeffrey Sachs to be a member of the Center, and he, as the director of the Earth Institute, was able to supply a closet-size office on Broadway for me to run the Center. When not a single foundation would provide support during those years of the somewhat depressed stock market, Jeff kept us afloat.

Our inaugural conference was held at Columbia on April 16–17, 2004—although some of us at the Center think of the 2001 *Festschrift* as the beginning of the Center's existence, as all or most of us were there. The title was "Capitalist Systems" and the speakers included Paul Volcker, William Baumol, Richard Nelson, Stanley Fischer, and Olivier Blanchard, Roman, as well as others (Clive Crook was there from the *Economist*). The speeches may not have been striking or stellar, but no other research center in the world would have done it. It was a start along the line of the Center's directions and themes.

Our second conference, "Aging Baby-Boomers and the Consequences for Dynamism, Prosperity, and Growth," was held in Reykjavik at the University of Iceland in June 2005. My student and frequent coauthor over the years, Gylfi Zoega was a coorganizer. Speakers included Bob Mundell and Jason Furman. We were off the ground and the wheels were lifted.

The Center showed what it could do with its third conference that was held in Venice, "Perspectives on the Performance of the Continent's Economies," cohosted with the Center for Economic Studies and the University of Munich. Hans-Werner Sinn was my coorganizer. Sinn presented a paper on continental performance, Andrzej and Roman presented on continental thought, Luigi Zingales presented on continental industrial organization, and I presented on continental values. The dinner party under the stars with the Venice Canal and the Guggenheim Museum below and guests including Mario Draghi and Martin Wolf was a night never to be forgotten. We ultimately published the conference volume, *Perspectives on the Performance of the Continent's Economies*, with MIT Press in 2011.

The Center needed much more space and autonomy than Jeff would have been prepared to provide. Fortunately, with the announcement of the Nobel Prize, our situation changed like night to day. Within days, I was paid a visit by Peter Jungen, the well-known, cosmopolitan, and energetic German businessman. Amazed by the Center's closet-like office and its penniless coffers, he quickly made an agreement with Columbia's new president, Lee Bollinger, in which Peter would give support to the Center for some time and Columbia would find suitable office space.

Amidst the years of waiting for that space, the Western world was shaken by the 2008 Great Financial Crisis. The U.S. banks and other financial entities had grossly overextended their lending and grossly underestimated the false representations of the borrowers. The Fed could do little to stop the consequent financial contraction throughout the Western world that followed and the end result—the Great Recession. The world was shaken by this crisis, a crisis originating some sixty blocks down Broadway.

The Center was present at the crisis. Its fourth annual conference, cohosted with the Council on Foreign Relations, "The Dynamism of U.S. Capitalism: Where Are the Weaknesses? Where Are the Main Threats?" on November 14–15, 2007, came too late to address widely the faults of the financial sector. And then the Center's fifth annual conference, "Economic Dynamism and Inclusion," held at the Club de Industriales, Mexico City, November 24, 2008, had to address problems in Mexico.

The Center, however, ultimately rose to the matter with two impressive conferences. The first was its sixth annual conference, "Emerging from the Financial Crisis," held at Columbia on February 20, 2009. Christine Lagarde and Paul Volcker gave the principal addresses. The central banker and long-time friend Lucas Papademos gave a speech on regulating the new financial sector. The second was its seventh annual conference, "Post-Crisis Economic Policies: Ideas for Restructure," organized by my friend and supporter Peter Jungen and held at the original Berlin offices of Deutsche Bank in Berlin, December 11–12, 2009. If any conference could compete with the conference in Venice, this was it. A number of banking figures and monetary experts were there, among them Bob Mundell and Paul Volcker, who gave the dinner speech. We celebrated over drinks in a space looking out at the four-horsed chariot atop the Brandenburg Gate.

In late summer 2010, the space was ready! It was superb, with a great line of windows looking out toward the Manhattan skyline. Lee kindly came over to wish us well in our mission on the occasion of the grand opening. The past decade had been full of wonderful times—and a major crisis. Now, I was excited about what I was hoping to achieve in the next decade.

8

THE GREAT WAVE OF
INDIGENOUS INNOVATION,
MEANINGFUL WORK, AND
THE GOOD LIFE

At the dawn of a new decade, the glow of the Nobel Prize had dimmed, and the plan to build and ultimately to test a new economic theory was already in full swing. I had been drafting a book introducing that theory in a somewhat historical framework for a little more than two years—since September 2008—and was intent on completing it with as little delay as possible. The working title was "Dreams and Glories," later titled *Mass Flourishing*. Part I of the book had been completed, Miranda Featherstone had edited it and, when she became the Center on Capitalism and Society's administrative manager, my new assistant, Francesca Mari—another Harvard literature major—did the editing.

Then something extraordinary came up—something that may have slowed down completion of the book a bit but widened interest in the book before and after its publication. In early January 2010, I was invited by Chen Fashu, a Chinese philanthropist, to be dean of the New Huadu Business School he was creating in Fuzhou, the capital of China's Fujian Province— an invitation that was intriguing and even exciting. Later that month at the World Economic Forum in Davos, Switzerland,

I ran into Lee Bollinger and asked him whether Columbia had a rule against taking on such a second job for a few years. He said there wasn't.

I received the green light and found that my time in China would be compatible with continuing to progress at a satisfactory rate with my new manuscript. I was happy to embark on this uncharted voyage. The signing ceremony in March was soon set up in Beijing.

The morning signing went smoothly and the New Huadu Business School was airborne. In the afternoon, Jun Tang, Chair Chen's lieutenant and previously the head of IBM in China, gave a speech on the mission of New Huadu filmed by all the television networks. He remarked to me on his way out that in a few hours all of China and the whole world, too, would know about the new school. And indeed, the school gradually became known in China. The groundbreaking ceremony took place on June 13 on the campus of Minjiang Unviersity where the New Huadu school building was to be built. Some of us gathered at the ground-site where construction had already started to engage in some ceremonial shoveling of dirt under a half-dozen umbrellas shielding us from a driving rain. It was an extraordinary event and reflected the extraordinary determination driving creation of the new school. It was also a memorable beginning of a new venture.

MEMORIES OF CHINA

The Business School—including its recently appointed president, Zhiyi He, and the professoriate—looked to me not to help with the curriculum (although I felt I did have an influence on what the school ought to prepare themselves to do), but rather to bring the emergence of the school to the attention of the business community and the government in Fujian Province China. Zhiyi set an example of dedication to the rest of us, traveling for a month all over Fujian Province to interview prospective enrollees.

Increasingly, the learning was two-way. In his autobiography published around 1700, the noted Irish–French economist Richard Cantillon was struck by the extraordinarily hard-working Chinese he saw during his visit to Shanghai. But that had not prepared me for the energy and expertise I observed in the Chinese firms I visited. Their zeal—and know-how (to use that 1838 American term)—largely accounted for the gains they had made in productivity and market share in world markets. This was made concrete one day when it was arranged for me to stop by a factory manufacturing a myriad number of zippers. In a chat over tea at the end of the tour, I remarked that the zipper was named after the sound it made when used, adding that the innovator lived in New York City. "Yes," the company head said, "we know the family very well. They live in Florida now." This industry, like a great many industries, had competition but also interchange and cooperation, in which Chinese firms had become an important part.

After some time, I started to feel a need to inject into my speeches to Chinese audiences my developing thesis—initially applied to the advanced economies of the West—on the importance of having an economy full of firms engaged (or open to becoming engaged) in indigenous innovation. In the Chinese economy, to be sure, many firms already had conceived and developed new methods or new products or both. On tours of Chinese industry in 2012, I had been impressed by the advanced robots that were developed and used in a factory I visited there. I suggested firms all over China ought to be keen on coming up with new ideas for new products and methods.

As the Business School got to be somewhat known in China and the Center on Capitalism and Society, too, it was natural that they would collaborate in some project. In March 2013, we organized a special conference, "China's Next Decade," held in Beijing. I took the opportunity to present my argument for widening innovation in the economy. Glenn Hubbard, former chair of the Council of Economic Advisers and dean of Columbia's Business School, spoke at the conference, as did Amar Bhide and Richard Robb. Raicho Bojilov presented a paper on career choice and education in nourishing innovation.

I had been given other opportunities to speak in China before New Huadu and after. Around 2001, I had given a lecture—my first in China—in Beijing at the invitation of Justin Lin, at an estate of Peking University. On our way back to the city's center in his car, I asked him why the bicyclists on the road were smiling. "It has something to do with the rise in their incomes," he said. Around 2004, Lu Mai, who had become a leader of the China Development Research Foundation, a newly created institution in Beijing, came to my office at the Center to urge me to give a presentation at the upcoming annual conference of the China Development Forum. That was the beginning of our long friendship.

At the 2005 meeting of the Beijing Nobel Conference, Bob Mundell, who had invited me, and I were sitting next to each other at the dinner that evening. Bob commented that "the reporters have code names for the speakers." When I asked him if he knew what my code name was, he said: Deep Thinker, Tobin's Traitor. Of course, I hadn't betrayed Jim. I had only qualified and gone beyond Jim's Keynesian beliefs.

In this same decade—around 2010—I gave an evening lecture on capitalism and socialism at Peking University, the Chinese university that John Dewey, renowned Columbia professor of philosophy and education, helped to build around a century earlier. The huge auditorium was crammed with students, some of whom seemed to be hanging from the ceiling of the hall. The atmosphere was electric, made more so by the intent interpreter, Amy Lin. Although most interpreters would stop the speaker after every sentence, she would let me read an entire paragraph from my prepared notes, then after furiously taking notes on my paragraph, she would recite it in Chinese. The questions after the talk were also excellent. This was perhaps the most exciting event in my classroom life.

Over the decade, I became more involved in China as a whole, beginning in 2012 with my participation in the Boao Forum, held annually in Hainan Province and aimed at providing a platform for Asian business leaders similar to the World Economic Forum in Davos. In addition to the speeches, it was a pleasure to be on the platform with Zhou Xiaochuan, the long-time head of China's central bank, and in the following year on the platform with William Rhodes, a former chair and CEO of Citibank.

I was invited to join a governmental entity, the State Administration of Foreign Experts, that was under the aegis of Premier Li Keqiang. I gave two talks at their annual meetings—one in a cavernous space in the Great Hall of the People. It was on that occasion in the autumn of 2013 that I first met Premier Li. In a photo shoot, while extending my right hand I handed him with my left hand my new book, *Mass Flourishing*. "I have read this book!" he exclaimed. "But I want you to have this autographed copy!" I replied. We were off to a good start. We were always glad to see each other at similar events.

I also had interchanges with officials in Fujian Province. Thanks, in some part, to such interactions, I was honored with the Government of China Friendship Award in 2014 in a large gathering of other awardees. It was a warm occasion, brightened by the congratulations of Premier Li.

In these years, Viviana and I had the good fortune to have two private meetings over dinner with Premier Li and others. In the first, he asked me—with real curiosity—who my favorite American philosophers were. I named Charles Peirce and William James. I was relieved to have remembered Peirce, whom Li had evidently read. He seemed pleased, and we went on to touch on a few other subjects. When the conversation of an hour was over, I felt fortunate to have had this meeting.

A year or so later, we met over dinner again. This time, he was delighted over a recent advance in China's economy—a step forward that he was instrumental in pushing through. Proudly, he showed me data on the surge of start-ups in the economy and appeared to expect an increase of entrepreneurial initiative in the Chinese economy. I expressed the expectation that some of these start-up firms might launch innovations— innovations of their own conceiving. He had read enough of *Mass Flourishing*, so he knew what I was thinking, but he was reticent on that score. For the time being, it appeared, he would be content to have more entrepreneurs marketing the innovations of others. How sad that China has now taken a very different direction.

A NEW THEORY OF INNOVATION, MEANINGFUL WORK, AND GROWTH

Mass Flourishing, written over a period of nearly five years, was published by Princeton University Press in August 2013. (The Chinese translation by Citic appeared that same month; the French translation by Odile Jacob and the Spanish translation by RBA Libros were released in 2017.) It was truly my *magnum opus*, as Esa Saarinen, the Finnish philosopher, had said.

The book introduces the concept of indigenous innovation, meaning the kind of innovating that might bubble up within a nation. This innovating draws also on people's observations—thus, their private information and their personal knowledge—as well as their creativity and originality. One might wonder whether this new theory had already been formulated in the forgotten past. But no such formulation has come to mind. One might suspect that Frank Knight in his 1921 book *Risk, Uncertainty, and Profit* had at least mentioned, if not proclaimed, that the would-be innovator faces uncertainty in the quest for profit, but no such mention appears in Knight's text. (The word "innovation" is used in a footnote on a quite different context.)

In the past, Friedrich Hayek, leading the Austrian school, introduced imperfect information to economics in the 1930s, and Michael Polanyi, the Hungarian philosopher-chemist, brought up "personal knowledge" in the 1950s. (I wished I had met him at his lecture on the subject at Yale, but I was away at MIT.) Although important, neither of these works were aimed at providing a theory of innovation.

Hayek makes it clear in a 1945 paper that he is discussing *adaptations*, as he calls them, to "changing circumstances"—not what is widely called "innovation."[1] Unlike innovations, adaptations have an air of predictability. They do not require an intuitive leap but are instead repercussions that would take place sooner or later. They do not stop if circumstances should stop changing. Innovations (from *nova*, Latin for new), in contrast, are not determinable from current knowledge and information, and thus unforeseeable. Being unforeseen, an innovation may be disruptive. They are the happenings to which adaptions adapt and "cumulatively they drive the economy's 'practice' on a path to ports-of-call that would otherwise have gone unseen."[2]

Polanyi, in his 1958 book *Personal Knowledge*, is clear from the first sentences that his attention is focused on the scientist in a laboratory aiming to add the "scientific knowledge," not the person in the economy considering an attempt at innovation. He writes, "This is primarily an enquiry into the nature and justification of scientific knowledge. I want to establish an alternative ideal of knowledge."[3] Nevertheless, one might find a broad parallel between Polanyi's view of researchers working in laboratories and my view of innovative people working in the nation's industries, which I described in *Mass Flourishing*. Of course, there are some commonalities between a theorist's work in some field and another theorist's work in some other field.

As I came to see while writing *Mass Flourishing*, the three main elements in indigenous innovation are the human capabilities at work, the desires of the nation's people that enlist these capabilities, and the distinctive rewards of the exercise of these capabilities.

Imagination and Creativity

The key premise of this new theory is that people generally possess imagination and creativity—not everyone, of course, any more than everyone is able to see and hear. This was an uncommon premise in economics, to say the least. (A premise of my paper "Population Increase," that a global increase in population would increase the generation of new ideas, was also uncommon.[4]) Basing a theory of economic growth, even a theory of the experience of life itself, largely on creativity was something new under the sun. The prevailing theory had long been based on discoveries of explorers, frontiersmen, and venturesome merchants or the results of scientists and experimenters.

As my draft of the book was getting started, I stumbled on stunning evidence of the possession and expression of creativity. Researchers at the University of Tübingen had recently unearthed some workable flutes fashioned from bones made by the cave dwellers that colonized Europe thirty-five thousand years ago, as Nicholas Conard and colleagues discovered and reported in the science magazine *Nature* in 2009. No evidence suggested that they had stumbled on the sole cave in Central Europe or even the whole of Europe possessing such talent and desire. Evidently, *Homo sapiens* were exercising imagination and displaying creativity as far back as a thousand generations.[5] This fortified considerably some of the themes that would constitute the thesis of the book.

The main advance in understanding provided by the cave discovery is that people cannot be said to lack creativity—contrary to much if not most economic thinking. Participants in the early economies, it appears, did not generally lack the desire to create—they invented and tested some things for their own use or enjoyment, such as the flute that Conard found. The early peoples had not organized enough to aim at creating new things for use in societies, nor had the early economies acquired the attitudes and institutions that would enable and encourage attempts at innovation.

If creativity and imagination are common in a nation, it may be that in those parts of the West where innovation was bursting forth—the United States from 1870 to 1970 and both Germany and France for a shorter time—it was these talents and powers among a wide number of the nation's people that were fueling the take-off of those countries into sustained innovating (to borrow Walt Rostow's image). These talents and powers enabled that stupendous innovating. But what was it that was sparking the fire that lights the fuel? What was driving the dynamism that drew on the talents and powers of the people?

Dynamism

It is clear that economic institutions were not the force behind this immense and unprecedented innovating—they were only necessary tools. The institutions of the market economy and capitalism had come into being years, even centuries, earlier, and they only facilitated the new phenomenon. The thesis of *Mass Flourishing* is that this innovating sprung from large numbers of people stirred by an emerging ethos—the spirit of the time and its leading figures. This spirit lit the sparks that lit the imagination of the people.

My book argues that, although some innovations were the result of the various sorts of discoveries outside the economy, the phenomenon of sustained innovating in a nation—its *indigenous* innovation—has generally derived from a desire among the people to innovate—typically, people already engaged in the economy. Similarly, "grassroots innovation," with which the book is concerned, came out of a desire of people, including "ordinary people," to create the new and see its use. The term *dynamism* often appearing in the book is shorthand for an outsized appetite and capacity for this indigenous innovation.[6]

The book further argues that this "dynamism" is generated by a compound of deep-set forces: the drive to change things, a receptivity to new things and, above all, a readiness to imagine and create. Of course, little innovation could result without enabling institutions such as a legal system. The advent of such dynamism set people in business thinking whether there could be a better way of doing something or a better thing to do. The result was the "modern economy," which brought a metamorphosis. Participants, who were apt to be struck by new commercial ideas, were turned into investigators and experimenters who manage the innovation process:

> A modern economy turns all sorts of people into "idea-men" . . . [It] is a vast *imaginarium*—a space for imagining new products and methods, imaging how they might be made, imagining how they might be used. Its innovation process draws on human capabilities not utilized by a pre-modern economy. This view is radically different from Schumpeter's 1912 thesis that innovation draws on the capacities of entrepreneurs to organize the projects made possible by *outside discoveries*. The human appetite and capacity he spoke of were "hustle" and the determination to "get the job done."[7]

The emergence of this dynamism and the resulting "imaginarium" raises the question of what exactly brought them into being—in those nations where they emerged.

There was never any shortage of explanations for the stunning outpourings of innovation in the West circa 1870. Abraham Lincoln exclaimed over the new feeling he witnessed in his 1858 tour of the country: "Young America has a great passion—a perfect rage—for the new."[8] Yet Lincoln did not have a sense of what lay behind the urge of people in various activities in the economy to conceive "the new" (and, for that matter, the urge to buy new things). Similarly, Frank Taussig, a well-known Harvard economist of his time, credited much of America's prowess to "Yankee ingenuity"—as if their inventiveness came from some genetic advantage.[9] He did not explain what generated the exercise of ingenuity—or why it was generated more in the

United States than all or most other countries. My book also points to the "modern experience" arising in the nineteenth century and continuing well into the twentieth century—the ceaseless change, the endless problem-solving, the pleasure of encountering the new, and much more, including modern music and modern art.

Values and Knowledge: Key Causal Forces

How, then, can the phenomenon of the modern societies—with their modern economies exuding high dynamism—be explained? "What makes modern economies modern?"[10] What are—or were, at any rate—the main drivers, the sources, the fuel mix?

In the thesis of *Mass Flourishing*, the formation of new ideas—new things to produce and better ways to produce—is fueled by the right values. A cultural shift in human history provided the energy needed for the emergence of the modern economies:

> The Western world came to acquire—in some nations and to a varying degree among those nations—a set of *values* that became the *ethos* of the modern economies, thus the spirit behind dynamism. This ethos that built up was part humanism and part modernism. In the countries where these strands reached a critical mass, they sparked the creation of a modern economy. . . . (It does not matter that the earliest of the elements of the new culture emerged some centuries earlier, as long as other crucial elements were more recent.)[11]

High dynamism derives largely but not solely from people (including businesspeople) brought up to use their imaginativeness and insightfulness to achieve a new direction; people at work driven by their desire to make their mark; people in venture investing willing to act on a hunch; and many end-users—consumers or producers—with the willingness to pioneer the adoption of a new product or method whose expected value is not knowable beforehand. This in turn requires the presence in people of aspiration, curiosity, and the desire for self-expression.[12] Thus, a modern economy requires a society that embraces modern values.

Modernist values include attitudes toward others: readiness to accept change desired by colleagues, eagerness to work with others, a desire to compete, and a willingness to take initiative. Other modernist attitudes are the desire to create, explore, and experiment; to overcome challenges; and to be engaged in one's work. Behind these desires is a need to exercise one's own judgment, to act on one's own insights, and to summon up one's own imagination. It is a spirit that views the prospects of unanticipated consequences that may come with voyaging into the unknown as a valued part of the experience.[13]

All this modernism stands in broad contrast to traditionalism with its notions of social harmony and of service to others and family. Under traditional values, individuals are more often made subservient to a group and corporatist economies are more likely to form. Solidarism and social protection, both features of a corporatist economy, are not conducive to high dynamism, or innovation for that matter, largely because these features place more value on conformism than over creating the new. But it is not untypical among the societies regarded as modern to find elements of traditionalism as well.

It would be hard to resist conveying the history of the modern values—the values often referred to as humanism—that played a key part in the thesis of *Mass Flourishing*. The book sees these values as fitting into three categories: individualism, vitalism, and self-expression.

There was first the rise of *individualism*. This individualism sprung up with the Renaissance in which Giovanni Pico della Mirandola wrote that since human beings were created by God in his image, they must also share in some degree God's capacity for creativity. Thus, individualism inspired people to carve out their own personal development. Similarly, Martin Luther's call for members of the Christian church to read and interpret the Bible for themselves reflects two essential aspects of individualism: using one's own judgment and thinking for one's self. Later, Voltaire, especially in his 1759 work *Candide*, championed further aspects of individualism: economic independence and rejecting conforming with convention.[14]

No less important was the rise of *vitalism* that swept from Italy through France, Spain, and Britain in less than a century during the Age of Discovery. This quality was pronounced in the lives of the great figures of early modernity: Benvenuto Cellini (a great sculptor and subject of a Berlioz opera), who was bent on achievement and success; Michel de Montaigne, who chronicled his inner life and personal growth or "becoming" in his *Essais*; Miguel de Cervantes, who wrote in *Don Quixote* of characters stuck in a place without challenges and going so far as to hallucinate them to find the vitality of a fulfilling life; and Shakespeare, who portrayed the interior struggle and courage of his protagonist in *Hamlet*.[15] All these figures exhibited in their work the vitality that had become part of modern life.

Also important was the emergence of a widespread desire for *self-expression* that manifested in a venturesomeness that had not been exhibited before on so wide a scale. It was exemplified early on by Daniel Defoe in *Robinson Crusoe*, the story of a young man showing his independence by embarking on a sea voyage. Increasingly, composers such as Claudio Monteverdi and Henry Purcell and painters such as Claude Monet and William Turner sought in their works to express themselves through the works they created.

Yet the desire to innovate is not enough to create innovations—that is, new methods and new products that are commercially successful. Possessing the right values is necessary for an outflow of innovations but not sufficient. The desire to introduce a better device in the production process, for example, or possibly a better product to produce, will not be realized until a method of production is conceived. Enter the Enlightenment.

The Enlightenment brought in the last half of the eighteenth century the first insight into what is needed to devise a new method of producing. The philosopher David Hume argued that theoretical imagination is the key to advances in theoretical knowledge: In his 1748 *An Enquiry Concerning Human Understanding*, he explains that new knowledge does not spring from sheer observations of the world and existing ideas. Our knowledge is never a completely closed system, so originality may break into it. New knowledge starts from imagining how parts of the system not yet studied might work. (Such imaginings may be sparked by a discovery but they do not require one.)[16]

In early America—a land with growing numbers—Thomas Jefferson likewise advocated an economy filled with participants free to operate their own proprietorships engaging in grassroots entrepreneurial endeavors. This individualism, vitalism, and self-expression became part of the West's core beliefs. Yet Jefferson went further:

> With his imperishable phrase "life, liberty, and the pursuit of happiness," he put two propositions into the minds of contemporary Americans: One is the notion that every person has the moral right to seek his or her fulfillment. . . . The other notion,

later developed by Søren Kierkegaard and by Friedrich Nietzsche, is the existential idea: a real life can come only through one's own endeavors. We may or may not find this "happiness," but we need to pursue it. These two propositions epitomize what we often call modernism. They are inimical to the ideas of traditionalism, which made the individual subservient to the group.[17]

The twentieth century saw the emergence of philosophers of vitalism. In what he called his "flux-philosophy," William James argues the excitement of fresh problems and new experiences are at the heart of the good life. While Henri Bergson, in his 1907 book *Creative Evolution*, conceived of people energized by *élan vital* (a current of life) and wrote of the transformation—the process of "becoming" that people undergo when intensely involved in challenging projects.[18]

Over the nineteenth century, as these new values began to permeate society, they resulted—quite directly for a great many participants—in the emergence of a change in the character of the economy. In businesses, there were increased levels of "zeal," as Gustav Cassel noted in his 1924 book, *Theory of Social Economy*, and that zeal may have spurred further investments, thus delivering a further rise of the capital stock. More important, the urge to venture into new ways of producing and new things to sell brought to the United States and several other nations a high rate of indigenous innovation—again, that is innovation not dependent upon unremitting discoveries of navigators and scientists (and vastly more important than the flow of such discoveries). This innovation—typically permeating a nation's entire economy—brought unprecedented economic growth (measured by growth of total factor productivity, TFP) for decade after decade starting as early as the early 1870s and continuing up to the early 1970s.

The rewards deriving from the distinctive and ever-new experiences arising in more and more businesses went beyond the profits earned—and ultimately the higher wages that generally followed over the nineteenth century. For a great many people in those nations that held the new modern values that fueled indigenous innovation, the arrival of these values brought about a profound change in the nature of work. The mental stimulation, the opportunity for new ventures, and the excitement of the unknown all nourish the innovator—all of those can outweigh the likelihood of failed attempts.[19] In the terminology of the present day, large numbers of people were flourishing in their work.

Flourishing, Not Just Prospering

This *flourishing* in a modern society comes from the experience of the new: new situations, new problems, new insights, and new ideas to develop and share. Clearly, flourishing on a massive scale requires broad involvement of people in the processes of innovation: the conceiving, developing, and spreading of new methods and products—all of which are part of the process of indigenous innovation from the grassroots up.

Such an economy presents a different world—a world that is more than competing in free markets. It is rich in jobs offering a sense of agency: people taking responsibility and exercising initiative. Only in the modern nations might there be the possibility of widespread venturing into the unknown.

Of course, the dynamic economy also offers greater *prospering*—in the sense of gaining increasing terms for what one does. It not only enables those who would have been prospering anyway to prosper at a faster rate. It may also enable some who would not otherwise be able to prosper.

In other terms, a reward arising in the dynamic economies of the modern societies—a reward widespread from the 1820s in Britain through the 1960s in the United States to Germany and France soon after—was the *experience* of living the so-called good life that nineteenth- and twentieth-century philosophers had conceived, that of not just "doing well"—not just making money.

In essence, then, the thesis of *Mass Flourishing* is that a new sense of the possibilities of life—possibilities beyond those of working, saving, and investing for security and enjoyment—provided the spark that fired the modern economies with the unprecedented experiences those economies would bring. People with vitalism, thus adventurousness, brought to their nation's economy the dynamism that generated indigenous innovation on a wide scale, and hence increased economic growth in the nation—thus lifting many out of poverty. Modern economies arose despite resistance to them.

Furthermore, many people able to participate in the process of conceiving a new method or even a new product might have a sense of being engaged in meaningful work. By the middle of the twentieth century, people in most modern economies spoke of "job satisfaction," understanding that rewarding work provides large satisfaction that is at least as important as the satisfaction of gaining or possessing large wealth. Work and careers were enlivened. Businesspeople of all sorts could see themselves as succeeding through the exercise of their creativity and imagination.

Mass Flourishing also tells the story of the struggles between modernism and corporatism as well as those between modernism and socialism. As the book comments, " 'The history of the World, Part II' is all about a seesaw battle between modernism and traditionalism—the endless struggle within the West from the early 1800s to the [late 1900s]."[20] Where modernism gained ground, traditionalism lost it, and a modern economy developed. Society flowered, as in Britain and the United States.

Yet, with the gradual revivals of traditionalism and gradual weakening of modernism at various times and in several Western nations, national economies drew back. Widespread flourishing had come nearly to an end everywhere—Germany by the 1920s, France by the 1930s, Britain by the 1940s, and the United States by the 1970s. (It would be interesting to study whether some of the recent political movements are correlated with a loss of modernism or a restoration of traditionalism.)

A Radical Departure

This theory of innovation, first presented in *Mass Flourishing* and further elaborated since then, is radically different from the standard theory of innovation. The concept of new economic ideas that are independent of advances outside the economy has been foreign to economists for decades. In the very early 1900s, the German Historical School, led by Arthur Spiethoff, made this explicit, holding that it was the discoveries of "scientists and navigators" that were the fundamental source—the *Ursprung*—of economic development.[21]

What the Austrian, Joseph Schumpeter, asserted in his 1911 classic, *Theorie der Wirtschaftlichen Entwicklung* and its 1934 translation, *The Theory of Economic Development*, is that the massive inflow of new products and methods springing up in some nations derived from the discoveries made by scientists and explorers, but required *entrepreneurs* (*Unternehmen*) to spot new opportunities, to judge what their commercial value might be, and perhaps to raise the capital to develop and market them. Here, there is nothing like creativity and imagination among businesspeople. In fact, Schumpeter exclaimed in his famous book that he had never met a businessperson with any creativity! On this crucial point, the theory outlined in *Mass Flourishing* departs radically from the theory introduced by the German Historical School (i.e., the German Spiethoff and the Swede Cassel) and developed by the Austrian Schumpeter.[22]

The logic of the innovation theory in *Mass Flourishing*, as readers will have grasped by now, is that a sufficient endowment of appropriate values in a nation can supply the necessary fuel for the dynamism needed to achieve the levels of indigenous innovation that are in turn necessary for widespread flourishing. Yet these necessary conditions are not sufficient, of course; adequate institutions are *also* necessary. The Western world was fortunate in possessing the invaluable institutions of political liberty and capitalism, with the former having begun in England with the Magna Carta and the latter having begun in fourteenth-century Hamburg and fifteenth-century Venice. It left aside the corporatism or authoritarianism, which greatly limits capitalism, that took hold in Mussolini's Italy, the Weimar Republic, Nazi Germany, the United States in the Great Depression, and Vichy France. (It should be noted that corporatism has regained strength in recent years.) Of course, liberty and capitalism are not sufficient on their own either—a huge point that many commentators and economists appear to be unaware of.

The thesis of *Mass Flourishing* provides, as I see it, a tenable, even persuasive, explanation of a remarkable event in human history—the century-long flourishing and rapid growth (of TFP) that arose in the West. From another perspective, however, this historical thesis points to a foundation on which to construct a formal theory of innovation, such as a full-fledged model of the innovation in a nation—a model that can be added to the set of existing models.

In moving toward a formal macroeconomic model, it may be helpful to visualize some procedures and institutions deployed in the processing of new commercial ideas and the selection of them for adoption. Ruminating on this, I thought of the medieval fairs, in which buyers chose which sellers to buy from. I had a vision one day of a storybook economy in which periodically some people who have been struck by an idea for a new thing to produce and sell travel to a traditional fair to "sell" their idea—moving from desk to desk in a large rectangular or circular pattern—each would-be innovator being interviewed by a producer.

The power of the germinal model that might be constructed, I thought, could be tested against the existing models—tested against the Spiethoff–Solow model, in which the driving force is scientific progress, represented by the passage of time (in the "forcing function," $f(t)$), and against the Aghion–Howitt model, in which the driver is the "research activities" of companies—or it can be introduced into a synthesis of models, leaving standard econometric methods to estimates the relative weight of each of the causal variables in the amalgamated model.[23] But the importance of a nation's values for its economic performance relative to that of other societies can be gauged in direct ways.

Estimating the Power of Modern Values

As my interest developed in the importance of culture— particularly, the role of certain values—I began to wonder whether data on values, compiled by household surveys, would give evidence, however flimsy, that the nations with high economic performance would be found to possess high levels of certain values. Without at least some indication that the performance of an economy, including the experience of work, appears to be connected (at least loosely) to attitudes reported in surveys, I doubt I would have gone forward with *Mass Flourishing*.

In 2005, I enlisted Raicho Bojilov and Luminita Stevens, doctoral students at Columbia, to search for data with which to gain a sense of the force of values on economic performance. With lots of data in hand, but few coming close to reflecting the modern values I would have liked, I proceeded to present some of the data and some of the conclusions in my paper, "Economic Culture and Economic Performance," in July 2006 at the Third Annual Conference of the Center on Capitalism held in Venice.

Two cultural variables scored well: Importance of Work, an attitude that is quite important for participation rates and unemployment rates, and Involvement (or Pride) in one's Work, which is important for productivity. In these respects, many of us think of the Europeans as painstaking craftsmen and of Americans as more practical. Thus, we would not be surprised if the Continent's average scores on these two counts were comparable or better than those of the comparators. Our survey finds that working people on the Continent are deficient on these two scores: "The data set shows that with respect to Importance of Work (c046), the Americans' score of 0.17 tops Germany's 0.11, Canada's 0.11 tops Italy's 0.08, and Britain's 0.07 tops France's 0.04. With respect to Involvement (c031), America's 2.87 tops Italy's 2.03, Britain's 2.80 tops Germany's 1.79, and Canada's 2.70 tops France's 1.74."[24]

"We may reasonably infer," I wrote, "from the empirical results detailed here that *some* cultural attributes really *do* matter for [a country's] economic performance in one or more respects . . . attributes a deficiency of which in a country would operate to pull down its economic performances in [one or more dimension]."[25] I also presented with Luminita some of the data and some of the conclusions I had drawn at the 2008 Lindau Nobel Laureate Meeting alongside the beautiful Bodensee.

Yet the statistical estimates of the effect of each of the attitudes, or attributes, on economic results, though not without interest, are in themselves of little importance. What is wanted is a sense of the importance of each of several main rivers, not that of each of the many tributaries of a great many rivers. It was necessary to simplify and hence to aggregate. I wondered what would happen if—to go to the other extreme—we construct an index of more-or-less modern values? Would we find that the nations whose modernism index is comparatively high has a measured performance level that is correspondingly high— as measured by one or more indicators—such as mean "job satisfaction"? For that matter, why not also consider an index of traditionalism?

In a 2012 working paper presented at the Center on Capitalism and Society, "Job Satisfaction: The Effects of Two Economic Cultures," Raicho and I adopt a procedure for the construction of an Index of Modernism in each of eighteen so-called advanced counties and then examine its relation to Mean Job Satisfaction. The estimated relationship was shown to be positive, as the thesis of *Mass Flourishing* predicts.[26]

Raicho suggested constructing an Index of Traditionalism, seeing traditionalism as standing in the way of modernism, and hence as an obstacle to the good things that modernism is capable of bringing, such as challenging work and opportunities. We found that the statistical relationship between the Index of Traditionalism and reported Mean Job Satisfaction among our data set of some 18 countries is *negative*. This lends credence to the belief expressed in the book that *modernism*, in nations where it is powerful, operates to boost job satisfaction—the job satisfaction that comes simply from pursuing the new, from exercising one's creativity, and from venturing into the unknown—both directly (as suggested previously) and indirectly in removing stifling traditions.

In sum, although the trinity of modern values in *Mass Flourishing*—individualism, vitalism, and the quest for self-expression—have not yet been satisfactorily measured, statistical estimates of the importance of a number of attitudes and beliefs give support to the thesis that modern values in a nation and any weakening of some traditional values are the source of high dynamism and thus of widespread, indigenous innovation.

The book's thesis—that a nation (especially a sizeable nation) with the right values is capable (institutions and other conditions permitting) of much innovation *beyond* what may be imported from abroad and what may be opened up by new scientific discoveries at home and abroad—is of enormous importance for Western societies. It means that a substantial loss of these values in a nation results not only in slower growth but also, and more important, a serious loss in the satisfaction people draw from their careers—their life's work.

TESTING MY THEORY OF INDIGENOUS INNOVATION

The publication of *Mass Flourishing* prompted the question of whether its central implication—that a major part of innovation in the United States, Britain, France, and perhaps the Scandinavian nations was indigenous in the sense of coming from the creativity within the workforce, not from advances in science and the discoveries of explorers, as the German

Historical School (including Schumpeter) held and econo-mists everywhere had accepted—might be subjected to one or more econometric tests.

In response, some two years later, I asked Raicho Bojilov, Hian Teck Hoon, and Gylfi Zoega to join with me in a research project to get some answers to the question. (Not surprisingly, the interests among the team led to related sta-tistical investigations and to some new modeling as well.) The end-result was *Dynamism: The Values That Drive Innovation, Job Satisfaction, and Economic Growth*, published in 2020 by Harvard University Press.[27] In a four-way phone call between New York, Reykjavik, Paris, and Singapore, we held almost weekly discussions on the recent research findings over the years 2017 to 2019. A great many of the most stimulating con-versations in my career have been those with Gylfi, Hian Teck, and Raicho. Every week I felt the stimulation of the week's challenge, puzzle, or surprise. I will always be grateful to them for their huge effort and for the joy I had in seeing evidence of the power residing in some modern values.

Three findings, at least, are of fundamental importance for my theory of innovation. The first of these comes out of Raicho's study of the national origins and transmission across countries of growth in TFP (based on historical data that had recently been gathered by the Bank of France). To quote: "A striking result, which justifies our emphasis on indigenous innovation, is that the exogenous innovation attributed to scientific discoveries is not of major quantitative importance."[28] That result is likely to be robust as further studies are made.

Some gratifying results emerged from Gylfi's statistical inves-tigation of the force of values in which the explanatory power of each variable in a set of values is estimated. He employed the method of canonical correlations proposed in the 1930s by Harold Hotelling (one of Columbia's greats), which is widely used in other social sciences. Gylfi finds that not only does "trust" matter—a value neither modern nor traditional, I think—but also "the willingness to take the initiative, the desire to achieve on the job, teaching children to be independent, and the acceptance of competition contribute positively to economic performance . . . measured by TFP growth, job satisfaction, male labor force participation, and employment."[29] It is a pity that more values of a modernist nature do not exist among the data we could find.

Some important theoretical findings came out of Hian Teck's analysis of the effects in a neoclassical growth model of two types of robots—additive and multiplicative. In a chapter on the growth effects of robots, he finds that "with the arrival of *multiplicative* robots—robots that are labor-augmenting—while the immediate impact is to cause the stock of conventional machines to fall . . . the real wage need not fall because of the off-setting labor-augmenting effect coming from the multiplicative nature of the robot."[30] In a more hopeful vein, he studies a two-sector model in which the creation of *additive* robots (robots that substitute for human labor) spurs investment in conventional machines, which stimulates indigenous innovation. Thus, once we depart from the first two-sector model to allow for indigenous innovation that raises productivity in the consumer goods sector, the inflow of additive robots is implied by the model to raise wage growth.[31]

As an economist studying the great Western nations, it has been gratifying to find evidence that values drive indigenous innovation and to show evidence that where there is relatively high indigenous innovation, there is relatively high job satisfaction. Additionally, we have found that where there is increased innovation, there is a relatively high proportion of responders saying they are "very happy."[32]

Unfortunately, the span of spectacular growth rates that had arisen first in the United States in the early 1860s and continued with little interruption—even in the Great Depression—came to an end in to the early 1970s. The Information Technology (IT) Revolution produced improved growth rates for a decade—from around 1995 to 2005—but spectacular growth did not return and still has not come back. Calculations by Raicho show that "cumulative growth" of TFP in the United States over twenty-year periods went from 0.381 in 1919–1939 to 0.446 in 1950–1970, and then down to 0.243 in 1970–1990 and to 0.302 in 1990–2010.[33] The statistic for one more twenty-year period, 1999–2018, is surely lower still. France, Germany, and Britain experienced even deeper plunges of TFP growth. (It is clear that the COVID-19 pandemic has done nothing to raise growth.)

This slowdown in the West has meant not only a slowing of growth in wage rates but also a discouraging decline of rates of return to investments and, as real rates of interest declined, a huge rise of share prices and housing prices. As a result, we have experienced an enormous rise in the existing value of wealth—with whatever effects that may have on the ambitions and dreams of working-age people. Out of such a long slowdown must come a deep loss of job satisfaction and thus human happiness.

No less important, this particular slowdown has consisted not of a more-or-less equal slowdown in each of the industries in the economy but rather a steep decline in most of the economy and ongoing or even new growth in some of the new industries, notably, the high-tech industries. Why, then, did the Western nations suffer a loss of much of the dynamism that had fueled the unprecedented innovation? The obvious hypothesis is that these nations experienced a major loss of the values needed to generate that dynamism—the modern values deriving from the ideas from Giovanni Pico, Martin Luther, and Cervantes to David Hume, Adam Smith, and onward to the nineteenth-century figures that had displaced to a degree the traditional values.

MIGHT GROWTH AND FLOURISHING BE REGAINED?

When *Mass Flourishing* closed its epilogue with its call for the lead nations of the West to regain "the genius of high dynamism—a restless spirit of conceiving, experimenting, and exploring throughout the economy from the bottom up leading to innovation"[34]—it was a call not only for rapid economic growth, thus widespread prospering, but also for the humanist goal of "mass flourishing," of meaningful jobs and rewarding work among people engaged in society's economy.

Thus, although low-paid workers have felt the frustration of seeing little or no rise in their real wage rates for decades, the better-paid workers have also felt the loss of job satisfaction over the fifty-year quasi-stagnation of the Western economies.

Can something be done—and without undue costs—to boost growth and increase flourishing in those Western nations that have felt decline? Perhaps so. But political and theoretical problems are getting in the way.

On the political side, a tangle of challenges has developed in the West calling for society's attention and the attention of policymakers. One of the oldest of these challenges is the abominably low wage rates among the lowest-paid workers. Another challenge is the problem of racial discrimination, gender discrimination, and discrimination against LGBTQ individuals in hiring and promotions. These latter challenges have long been difficult, because the evidence of discrimination may often be difficult to obtain, so there is plenty of room for more action on this matter. It may be that the talents among racial minorities, among women, and among LGBTQ individuals can play roles in getting the West out of its morass.

A new challenge has arisen in recent decades—most visibly in the United States and to varying degrees in Britain, France, and elsewhere in Europe. Many in the working class have relatively few skills suited to the information economy. Thus, the individuals who are earning relatively little resent the competition that comes from nonwhites and foreigners, resulting from immigration and from the long rise of education. Furthermore, many of these people might well be anxious over the stupendous rise of productivity in Asia, which has sent the terms of trade between the Westand East on a strong downward slide. Many others are anxious over advances in artificial intelligence. So, they fear an *absolute* decline of income and social position.

There is also, of course, the immense problem of global warming, more generally, climate change, which has already begun to do immense damage to the earth and the people on it. It already presents a huge challenge: to put a stop to further global warming and to roll back to a significant degree the recent warming. Yet a highly dynamic society could continue to exercise its innovative initiatives in the accustomed range of industries while directing other resources to renewable energy, conservation, and the like.

Another development is the massive monopolies that have grown up out of the IT Revolution. This is a source, although not the only source, of the semistagnation of recent decades in the United States and the other lead economies: Britain, Germany, and France. Among the consequences of this slowdown of productivity growth are businesses running into steeply diminishing returns to capital, resulting in deeply reduced rates of return, hence a sharp slowdown in the growth of both the capital stock and real wage rates, households facing meager real rates of interest on whatever savings they can accumulate, elevated rising prices of houses or any other assets they might like to buy, and—very important—a serious loss of job satisfaction.

In view of the manifold need for new governmental initiatives with one aim or another, then, it is obvious that Western nations would be hard pressed to meet all of these calls for government intervention as fully as needed. It is not likely that there will be nearly enough taxable capacity to meet all these needs. And meeting all of the shortfall with new public expenditures, subsidies, tax cuts, and resulting fiscal deficits would soon slow growth even more until the capital stock has reached a lower time-path, thus lowering the time-path of wages.

On the theoretical side, matters may be quite complex. For example, it may be difficult to assemble the present elements in the theory of growth and flourishing into an econometric model that could be used to identify the effects of changes in each of several instruments of policymaking on growth and flourishing. So, it would be quixotic to suppose we could identify the "optimum" setting of these instruments, as if we were agreed on the "social utility function" that is to be maximized. We might fail to hit upon a mix of policies that would prove to be a good mix, let alone the optimal mix.

Keynes in his *General Theory* was fortunate to identify a governmental instrument—public spending—that could plausibly serve to exert a counterforce on an aggregate demand level that had become depressed. That intuition proved right in America's Great Depression and such an intuition was to prove right many more times in the future—although such actions have not always delivered the result sought. In situations in which the emergence of unemployment had other causes—a decline of coal mining or steelmaking, to take one example—an increase of aggregate demand might be ineffective. In fact, it was not clear in the earlier years when Britain's unemployment was quite high that public spending would have been much help since much of any increase in demand might have spilled out to other countries, particularly given Britain's small, open economy.

In the present context, too, the theoretical intuition of some of us economists would suggest (if trained on the question at hand) that a number of policy actions surely exist that would encourage innovation. But what would those be? The nation's policysetters will need to gauge costs and benefits, and consider the trade-offs. Could society come to agree on a policy mix to adopt?

Yet there is always hope, as Dickens said. In a free society, it is the attributes of the people, such as their values, that largely determine their possibilities and their success. If these societies in the West were somehow to regain the values of the Renaissance and the Enlightenment or rediscover in themselves these values—or remove whatever has blocked a continuation of the mass innovating—the resulting rebirth would work miracles: Western nations would then regain rapid growth and widespread flourishing. And that could be expected to put an end to many of the social tensions that have engaged public discourse and depressed Western societies.

Moreover, if a firm that sought to win a new market and failed, but its employees experienced the rewards of participating in the project—if they have achieved personal growth or experienced the thrill of adventure in the process—then this flourishing would not be totally lost.

All this is something for society to hope for.

Moreover, *individuals* acting on their own *initiatives* can try to make something of their lives—a point that comes up next.

LOOKING BACK

Reflecting on my work over the past two decades, culminating in *Mass Flourishing* and *Dynamism*, I had a sense that its implications were important—although perhaps not more than (and perhaps less than) my role in putting the theory of unemployment on microeconomic foundations or my work on economic justice and on structural slumps. But in the past, I had always contributed to the theories conceived by others: Keynes's unemployment theory, Solow's growth model, Rawls's theory of economic justice, and even Hayek's view that consumption is contractionary. I was always building on someone else's theory, never building a theory of my own. With *Mass Flourishing*, I had at long last used my creativity—creativity we all have in differing and perhaps variable amounts—to build a new theory of a nation's innovation and the resulting happiness—a theory radically opposed to Schumpeter and the neoclassical theory of growth and working life. I felt a little like John Keats's Cortez, "silent on a peak in Darien."

The neoclassical perspective of Spiethoff and Schumpeter, incorporated to a large degree in the models built by Solow and Trevor Swan, no longer looks adequate to understand economic growth and—ultimately more serious—no longer a description of human *happiness* and how people generate it in the process of "making their garden grow." The activity of work is fundamental to that happiness, as Voltaire conveyed in his play *Candide*. One Sunday a few years ago, following a luncheon at home with friends, I had the joy of singing the final aria and duet from *Candide*, music by Leonard Bernstein and lyrics by Richard Wilbur, who perhaps taught Bernstein in his Harvard poetry class, in which Candide sings to Cunégonde, "Let us try before we die to make some sense of life. We're neither pure nor wise nor good;

we'll do the best we know; we'll build our house and chop our wood, and make our garden grow. And make our garden grow."

The story told in *Flourishing* and examined in *Dynamism* implies that economics ought not to stop at the standard theory with its elements of capital, employment, and national income; its trade-offs between work and leisure and between present and future consumption; and its models of choice behavior. And it ought not to stop at understanding the causes and effects of unemployment, growth, innovation, economic justice, and the other phenomena under its lens. It ought to venture *outside* those standard fields (and no doubt others) to explore an unchartered realm: the manifold rewards of work—the personal growth that comes from participating alongside others, the satisfaction of succeeding at something, the excitement of creating something, and the self-discovery that comes from overcoming obstacles, engaging in one's work, taking initiative, venturing into unknown, and thrilling to the new. In his book *Willful*, Richard Robb depicts "employees and entrepreneurs caught up in the 'sport' of economic life."[35]

I would point out that these experiences of work are not simply key inputs to indigenous innovation in a nation's economy and thus a source of its economic growth. They are goods in themselves—and invaluable goods at that. It is imaginable that an economy may develop in which the sophisticated firm regularly offers full-time employees working in the office a space in which to use their imagination to conceive new things, much as a firm might offer a recreation room to practice sports. An orientation toward creativity would be common and even widespread. The provision of this facility to employees would be a part of their benefits.

An acceptance of all this by economists will undoubtedly lead to the acceptance of a major broadening of standard economic theory. Most work, for example, will appear as a source of utility, not as a major source of disutility. And such an extension of the standard theory can be expected to bring about a wider set of conditions on which present-day economic policies are based and to bring about a new set of economic policies aimed at recognizing the widely neglected rewards of which the economy is capable of producing. The rough simplification that most people work to go on living would be replaced by the notion that most people live to go on working.

This theory that I conceived and managed to develop has given me far more satisfaction than any of the other contributions I have made to economics. Nothing I have done before has been so close to my heart. And I have the feeling that creating the new and experiencing the good life are irresistible concepts that have been working their way into present economic thought. Moved this past November by a performance at the Met of *Die Meistersinger*, I commented—voice choking—to Eric Maskin, "Wagner struggled for acceptance of his new music, and I've struggled for acceptance of my theory of innovation."

Eric replied: "Yes, but Wagner won and so have you."

EPILOGUE

I t has been a privilege and mostly a joy to have been living a life of the mind for some sixty years beginning at the RAND Corporation, then moving to Yale's Cowles Foundation with excursions to the Massachusetts Institute of Technology and the London School of Economics, next heading to the University of Pennsylvania, and finally—for fifty of those years—ending at Columbia University. It has also been an extraordinary experience to tell this story of "personal struggles and academic politics."[1]

At various places in these memoirs, I have mentioned my excitement over my early successes in the 1960 and 1970s, the later ones in the 1990s, and what for me was the deeply rewarding success of the past two decades. In the closing pages of the last chapter of these memoirs, I tried to convey my deep satisfaction in conceiving a new theory from the ground up.

Stepping back from this account, however, I see that some further observations are needed, although it is not possible to do justice to all of these subjects in just a few pages.

A NEW AND WIDENING CIRCLE

Conceiving a new idea over weeks or months does not happen without support from within the community in which the person forming the new idea thinks and works—nor does the satisfaction of forming it. What has been satisfying in my work as an economic theorist has not simply been having the occasional idea, exciting though some of the ideas were, and gaining recognition for it, but also experiencing the competition and the sense of a quest alongside like-minded colleagues—a kind of team effort.

The sense of support coming from others—even if only from a few—is hugely important. After almost everything else has been forgotten, the personal exchanges stay in my mind. Few of us, if any, could have gotten far without a sense of support at an early age and a sense of rapport or appreciation among a circle of peers.

In the summer of 1954, when I had only begun to develop as some sort of thinker in economics, both Clarice Thorp and Emile Despres conveyed to me at the Merrill Center for Economics a feeling of encouragement that stayed with me for decades, no matter how few our meetings would be later on. As a graduate student and later as an assistant professor at Yale, I found encouragement from Willi Fellner and Gus Ranis. Willi gave me a private course in Hayek when I was in graduate school and continued to add to my knowledge about the Austrian school and the German Historical School when I was at Cowles. Gus and I bonded, traveling to a World Congress in Vienna in 1965 and driving from New Haven to Yankee Stadium, where we saw Mickey Mantle power a memorable drive toward right field that was blocked—thanks to the new park lights—from being the only out-of-the-park homer in the history of the stadium.

I drew on both their European backgrounds and their encouragement, and I was bolstered by their appreciation of my explorations and curiosity.

In later years, I met occasionally with Amartya Sen to talk a little about our work and, thanks to him, got to know John Rawls through whom I got to know Tom Nagel. It was hugely gratifying and encouraging to be a part of this circle they had started. There was not much that I did from the early 1970s to the late 1990s that did not draw on something I learned from them. I could feel Jack's appreciation of my work in our correspondence and the all-too-few meetings we had in New York— just as he could see my appreciation of his work in my writings. (A Rawls scholar, Larry Udell, told me in autumn 2019 that I appeared to be the economist Rawls read the most.) The importance to me of Jack's support was considerable.

In the past two decades, the support of my contemporaries has been deeply invaluable. I felt support from Paul Samuelson when he told me he kept his copy of *Rewarding Work* sticking out from his bookcase, from Roman Frydman when in a phone call he referred to my "legacy" of a micro-based macroeconomics, and from Richard Robb when he wrote in his book *Willful* that "with [his] project at the Center he intended to reformulate economics for the modern world . . . to describe 'real human beings who are not only acquisitive and risk averse but also inquisitive and adventurous and who sometimes feel the need . . . to leap into the unknown.'"[2]

By the 1990s, a new circle of economists had formed (rather like the Vienna Circle of the 1920s and the Cambridge Circus in the 1930s). Its members had broken free from one or another element of neoclassical theory, and many were influenced by the ideas of the modern philosophers, including Friedrich Nietzsche, William James, Henri Bergson, Karl Popper, and others. The striking departures in understanding trust and other phenomena in markets and elsewhere by Thomas Schelling were encouraging broader thinking in economics. My micro-macro work in the 1960s put me in this modernist circle—along with Sidney Winter. The further work by Roman Frydman in the 1970s and 1980s on expectations under the heading of "imperfect knowledge" put him in this circle, too. Joseph Stiglitz added to that knowledge with his models based on asymmetric information. George Akerlof and Robert Shiller entered the circle with their macro work in the 2000s on "animal spirits" and Bob further contributed with his later macro work in 2019 on the part that "narratives" played in pricing stocks. Richard Robb entered the circle with his radically new micro theorizing on people's "willful" decision-making, also published in 2019. Benjamin Friedman's work on the influence of the Enlightenment in 2021 made him one of us. There are surely other members of this modernist circle I have overlooked. These figures and other like-minded figures may never have been in the same room together, but, as I was looking back at this compilation, I was struck by the remark of Amartya Sen in his memoir *At Home in the World,* "We can have close friendships far beyond our immediate circles."[3]

The sense of shared orientation that this circle of theorists fostered was surely important to all of us in the continuing course of our work. Certainly, it was important to me to know that others had gone in these humanist and modern directions, and they, too, had to defend their work or suffer its neglect.

Listening to Jeffrey Sachs talk about the error of thinking that the natural rate is a constant, discussing notes that Pentti Kouri showed me on the "scope that real-wage rigidity would open up for real demand shifts to alter employment," and having an interchange with Joe Stiglitz on whether or not the "natural rate was as likely increasing with the real wage as decreasing"— and, no doubt, other ideas arising in the 1980s—all played some part in my development with Hian Teck Hoon and Gylfi Zoega of the employment theory in *Structural Slumps*.[4]

As the Center on Capitalism and Society at Columbia took shape beginning in 2001, Paul Volcker increasingly became an informal member—and a close friend. He chaired the round table at the end of our Inaugural Conference in 2004; he gave the luncheon speech at the Sixth Annual Conference following from the Great Financial Crisis, in February 2009, where Christine Lagarde and Lucas Papademos also spoke; and he gave the keynote speech at the Seventh Annual Conference, "Post-Crisis Policies," held in December 2009 at the 1880s offices of Deutsche Bank with a post conference party in the shadow of the four horses atop the Brandenburg Gate. In his last decade, I was fortunate to meet Paul often—almost to the end of his life. We enjoyed each other's spirit of independence. (I asked him one day over lunch whether he had left the Democratic Party. He replied instantly that "the party left me!") At Paul's memorial service in the Presbyterian Church on Madison Avenue, it seemed that everybody in economics, banking, and the art of government was there. A giant had gone, but his legacy remains.

Our work at the Center continued. My project to build a new theory of innovation was getting underway when Richard Robb and I met and began to have almost weekly conversations on economic theory, which continue to this day. To be able to discuss the questions arising in my project with someone having his knowledge—from Aristotle to Kierkegaard, Nietzsche, Fyodor Dostoevsky, and William James—gave me the confidence to go farther than I would have otherwise gone. We both value self-expression, and Jacques Barzun's *From Dawn to Decadence* is a favorite book we have in common. Richard was very helpful as I sought to characterize some of the satisfactions in the workplace drawn from indigenous innovating. Undoubtedly, *Mass Flourishing* would not have gone as far as it did without Richard's influence. (At a book party, he described his book *Willful* as a "prequel" to *Mass Flourishing*.)

In the excitement of that time, I felt that we—my coauthors in *Dynamism*, Richard and I—were part of a movement to wrest economic theory from the restrictions imposed by its long-held traditions. (Richard Sennett in his book *The Culture of the New Capitalism* was also part of that movement.) I sensed then that all of us in this movement share a high regard for the humanism emerging from the Renaissance that urged independence and personal voice, that called for engaging in work that offers a sense of agency, not the mechanical working lives postulated by neoclassical models. We share an admiration for living a life of exploration and creating the new—for a humanism that calls for increased attention to nonmaterial rewards. I knew at the time that we also share a high regard for the modernism that recognized that the actors in the economy (and the economists, too) do not possess nearly the full knowledge of the present or the future nor in all cases even the self-knowledge that would be of benefit.

The Center on Capitalism and Society made further steps in new directions when Richard Sennett joined in 2010 and Philip Howard joined in 2015. With Richard Robb and I leading the way, the Center became in the 2010s the place where much of this new work was developed or first presented. Our shared interests and the overlapping books we had written brought Richard and me together, much as they had brought Roman and me together decades ago. After *Mass Flourishing* came out in 2013, leaving to the future further statistical and econometric work to test its theses, Raicho Bojilov, Hian Teck

Hoon, and Gylfi Zoega joined me in a big research project at the Center from 2015 to 2019, which culminated in the publication of *Dynamism* in 2020.

The circle of thinkers I pointed to at the start of this epilogue has been expanding in the years following publication of the most recent trio of books *Mass Flourishing*, *Willful*, and *Dynamism*. From the early 2010s to the present, more and more thinkers understand that the innovation springing up in a nation derives largely from the people at large and that the good life involves (for most people) working with others to conceive new solutions and create new things or new services of value—either directly or indirectly through the economy to members of society.

It has been wonderful to see over the years the beginning of an acceptance among economists of the ideas of indigenous innovation, even innovating by "ordinary people," and the notion that the experience of work is integral to a good life—that in creating things we express who we are.

ENVISIONING THE FUTURE

This circle, if not overcome by some crisis or crises, can be expected to widen further over the present decade and perhaps the next. With such a sea change of thinking in the economics profession, the neoclassical theory that my generation of economists (and earlier ones) taught and applied—adjusting it only for the imperfect information of Keynes and the uncertainty of Knight—will be seen to be of little practical use for economists wanting to address, say, a further serious fall of job satisfaction or a secular slowdown of growth. When *Flourishing* closed its epilogue with a call for the lead nations of the West to regain their dynamism, it was a call for flourishing as well as for regaining significant economic growth.

A new kind of economics, or political economy—one that incorporates the flourishing brought by widespread involvement in innovating and problem solving—must be formalized to teach students something about what the economy is capable of delivering and how it functions. Neoclassical theory could still be brought to bear on such classic maladies as trade wars, Rawlsian injustice, and monopoly power, but this new economics would address the importance of indigenous innovating and the meaningful work that it brings.

For our own self-respect, we economists will have to expound and develop further an economics that recognizes the nonpecuniary rewards of *meaningful work*—the challenges and the achievements as well as the sense of participating in the economy, society's main project. In short, we will need an economics that incorporates the phenomenon of flourishing. With such an economics, we will put an end to the awful crassness sometimes found in our profession.

It has been a thrill to present in this book a history of my life's work—the legacy of my career as an economic theorist: better and fuller foundations for unemployment theory, a model of Rawls's just economy, an econometric test of Keynes versus Hayek, a rejection of Schumpeter's theory of innovation on which standard growth theory has rested, and the injection of meaningful work and the good life into economic theory.

It has been a particular delight in the course of writing these memoirs to take the younger readers of these memoirs on a tour of the "generations" of economic theorists in my time—the generation of Gottfried von Haberler, Joan Robinson, and John Hicks, all of whom I met; the generation of Paul Samuelson,

Kenneth Arrow, Thomas Schelling, and Robert Solow—all of whom I knew well—and what I think of as "my generation"— the generation of Robert Mundell, Amartya Sen, and Robert Lucas, all of whom I interacted with or reacted to. (Many other brilliant figures have emerged after them, of course.)

I have enjoyed recounting in these memoirs some of the memorable exchanges I had and comments I heard at one time or another with most, if not all, of these seminal figures in economic theory. Of course, it is the disagreements we had, not the areas of agreement, that were most interesting—and certainly the most fun. I hope that some of these interchanges and anecdotes have brought to life some of the great figures of the past and some of the controversies they sparked.

As I was conveying in this book my theory of people's exercise in the business world of their creativity to conceive new methods and new things, I became increasingly aware that in conceiving that new theory, I was using my own creativity. (The theory was not stumbled onto: it required imagination.) Some readers might therefore see this book as the story of my personal development more than a recording of my part in the controversies in economic theory over the past six decades—the story of my personal growth like a Thomas Mann *bildungsroman*. It would be gratifying if some of my readers were to take inspiration from my story.

I will be deeply gratified if this book's saga of the birth of my creativity theory of indigenous innovating—and, most of all, the rewards of work it brings to those engaged in that innovating— stimulates economists reading this book to join in the revolution that this new theory envisions. This book will have been worthwhile if its readers gain a greater sense of how far economic theory has come in the past 60 years and how much deeper its contribution to society may yet be.

With this story—of my interactions with economic theory—at an end, it might be wondered whether I will be setting out anew. I hope to go on observing the world and finding things to say about new developments as long as I can. I take some inspiration from the many writers and composers who worked on into their late years. At present, there appears to be no reason to stop. My expectation is that there will be new questions to address and, with luck, new ideas bringing the answers.

ACKNOWLEDGMENTS

Writing these memoirs got underway in early summer of 2020, not long after COVID-19 upended our lives—working in a small study at home without the convenience of my office and interacting with others from home through phone and video calls made it all the more difficult. The first draft was completed in September 2021 and, after the twentieth-anniversary conference and other matters at the Center on Capitalism and Society, the final draft was completed at the end of January. In view of the extraordinary difficulties to be overcome, I am more than usually grateful for those without whose support and help my writing the book would not have been possible.

It was no small thing that my wife, Viviana, helped in myriad ways almost daily with the project as I struggled to work at home after decades of almost never doing so—recollecting events and almost whole years in our lives together. She felt it when progress stopped or worries arose. The upside was that she and I could jump to celebrate immediately when something good happened. It is no exaggeration to say that in these difficult circumstances, the project could not have seen fruition without Viviana's support.

As the book began developing, I asked my colleague and close friend, Richard Robb, an economic theorist, statistician, and philosopher, if he would read chapters in draft. His comments gave me some needed encouragement as well as some needed corrections. Our rapport gave me a sense that I was on the right track—or, as it was the only track I knew, a sense that I was getting somewhere. In the last chapter and the epilogue, where I began to go further away from the orthodoxy of existing economics, Richard's support encouraged me to stick to my guns.

I can't imagine embarking on these memoirs without knowing that I could pass the editing and the research onto my assistant of more than five years, Catherine Pikula, a poet and *ikebana* artist, once a teacher of poetry at New York University and intern at Knopf. After my draft of each chapter, she spotted the many errors, factual as well as grammatical, and the effectiveness of the chapter as drafted. I doubt I would have got to the end without her contribution and patience. We gave whoops of delight as we reached completion of the first draft.

Also helping greatly was Lizzie Feidelson, administrative manager of the Center I direct, as well as a dancer and a writer—recently in the *New Yorker*. When COVID-19 forced me to work at home, Lizzie brought me the laptop and supplies I would need to write the book. When in the spring of 2021, my sabbatical over, I was teaching a senior seminar remotely while writing the book, Lizzie, who was managing the video call, exclaimed, "Ned, what a good teacher you are!" I treasured that boost as I faced the steep climb of writing chapter 8.

I want also to acknowledge the contribution of Christian Winting, editor at Columbia University Press, who encouraged me to bring up early in the book how very important the exercise of creativity was in my early work as an economic theorist, and how even more important the exercise of creativity was in my breaking loose from the perspective of the prevailing economic theory. Christian understood more than I did how revolutionary this book ultimately is.

How very fortunate I have been on my voyage.

NOTES

INTRODUCTION: FORMATIVE YEARS

1. Thorp's influence was such that, when difficulties arose in Germany, he was able to recruit and send over a team consisting of Kenneth Galbraith, Walt Rostow, and Emile Despres. Willard L. Thorp, interview by Richard McKinzie and Theodore A. Wilson, July 10, 1971, Harry S. Truman Library, Independence, MO.

2. Some of the students were interesting, too. A graduate student in economics at Yale, Fred Pryor, during a semester or more of doing research in East Germany, returned to tell his harrowing story. He had been arrested and held captive by the Stasi, the East German secret police, on suspicion of stealing secrets. His interrogators were particularly suspicious of what was going on in Room Q of the Yale Library where many of us did much of our reading for some of our courses. When Fred was finally released in a prisoner exchange, we listened avidly to his story and the Stasi's suspicion of what we were staging in Room Q. (The 2015 movie *Bridge of Spies* tells the drama of the negotiation and the cliffhanger of Fred's release.)

3. It was published in *Yale Economic Essays*, vol. 1, one of the newly funded journals of papers based on PhD dissertations.

1. BEGINNING MY CAREER: GOLDEN RULE OF SAVING AND PUBLIC DEBT

1. Edmund Phelps, "The Golden Rule of Accumulation: A Fable for Growthmen," *American Economic Review* 51, no. 4 (September 1961): 638–643.

2. For more on the Solow–Swan growth model, see Robert Solow, "A Contribution to the Theory of Economic Growth," *Quarterly Journal of Economics* 70, no. 1 (February 1956): 65–94; and Trevor Swan, "Economic Growth and Capital Accumulation," *Economic Record* 32, no. 2 (November 1956): 334–361.

3. Edmund Phelps, "The Accumulation of Risky Capital: A Sequential Utility Analysis," *Econometrica* 30, no. 4 (October 1962): 729–743.

4. Edmund Phelps, "The New View of Investment: A Neoclassical Analysis," *Quarterly Journal of Economics* 76, no. 4 (November 1962): 548–567.

5. A recent Amherst College video documents Frost's influence on Kennedy and the rift when Frost made a visit to Moscow. See *JFK: The Last Speech*, dir. Bestor Cram (Boston, MA: Northern Lights Productions, 2018).

6. The "excess burden" literature appears to begin with Jules Depuit and is part of the canon of A. C. Pigou, F. P. Ramsey, and others in the 1920s and 1930s.

7. The investment-output ratio fell to 15 percent in 1921, 16 percent in 1922, and 17 percent in 1923. See Òscar Jordà, Moritz Schularick, and Alan M. Taylor, "Macrofinancial History and the New Business Cycle Facts," *NBER Macroeconomics Annual* 31, no. 1 (2016): 213–263.

8. David Ricardo, *Principles of Political Economy* (London: John Murray, 1817).

9. I am thinking of Franco Modigliani, "Long-Run Implications of Alternative Fiscal Policies and the Burden of the National Debt," *Economic Journal* 7, no. 284 (December 1961): 730–755; Arnold C. Harberger, "Efficiency Effects of Taxes on Income from Capital," in *Effects of Corporate Income Tax*, ed. M. Krzyzaniak (Detroit, MI: Wayne State University Press, 1966), 107–117; and Peter Diamond, "National Debt in a Neoclassical Model," *American Economic Review* 55, no. 5 (December 1965): 1126–1150.

10. In neoclassical models, the growth path of wealth, shifted up by the increase of public debt, is also tilted down but not so much as to reach a new level below or at its initial level. In other words, wealth remains swollen although less than initially.

11. Edmund Phelps, *Fiscal Neutrality Toward Economic Growth: Analysis of a Taxation Principle* (New York: McGraw-Hill, 1965). A more readable exposition is my essay, "Fiscal Neutralism and Activism Toward Economic Growth," in *The Goal of Economic Growth*, ed. Edmund Phelps (New York: Norton, 1969) and reprinted in Edmund Phelps, *Studies in Macroeconomic Theory*, vol. 2, *Redistribution and Growth* (Cambridge, MA: Academic Press, 1980), 185–199.

12. Phelps, *Fiscal Neutrality*, 38.

13. Phelps, *Fiscal Neutrality*, 39.

14. Phelps, *Fiscal Neutrality*, 40. In the United States, though, as Gylfi Zoega has pointed out to me, the recent purchases of securities by the Federal Reserve operate to decrease wealth and thus to offset the growth of wealth that the Treasury is causing. The resulting fall of interest rates can be argued to drive up consumer prices to the point at which real cash balances held by the public are back down to their original level. At that point, private wealth has been reduced by the amount of the securities they had sold to the Fed. Students of monetary theory may remember just that argument in a classic by Lloyd Metzler—a paper studied in *Fiscal Neutrality*. See Lloyd Metzler, "Wealth, Saving, and the Rate of Interest," *Journal of Political Economy* 59, no. 2 (April 1951): 108.

15. Phelps, *Fiscal Neutrality*, 60.

16. Edmund Phelps, with Hian Teck Hoon, George Kanaginis, and Gylfi Zoega, *Structural Slumps: The Modern Equilibrium Theory of Unemployment, Interest, and Assets* (Cambridge, MA: Harvard University Press, 1994.)

17. Edmund Phelps, "The Fantasy of Fiscal Stimulus," *Wall Street Journal*, October 29, 2018.

18. Bela Balassa, *The Theory of Integration* (Homewood, IL: Allen & Unwin, 1961).

19. Gustav Ranis, *Development of the Labor Surplus Economy* (Homewood, IL: R. D. Irwin, 1964).

20. Edmund Phelps, *Golden Rules of Economic Growth* (New York: Norton, 1966).

21. Edmund Phelps, *Political Economy: An Introductory Text* (New York: Norton, 1985).

2. A NEW DIRECTION: UNCERTAINTY AND EXPECTATIONS

1. Frank Knight, *Risk, Uncertainty and Profit* (Boston: Houghton Mifflin, 1921).

2. Knight, *Risk, Uncertainty and Profit*.

3. Edmund Phelps, "The Accumulation of Risky Capital: A Sequential Utility Analysis," *Econometrica* 30, no. 4 (October 1962): 729–743.

4. Friedrich Hayek, *Prices and Production* (London: Routledge, 1933).

5. John Maynard Keynes, *The General Theory of Employment, Interest and Money* (London: Palgrave Macmillan, 1936).

6. Keynes, *General Theory*.

7. John Hicks, "Mr. Keynes and the 'Classics'; A Suggested Interpretation," *Econometrica* 5, no. 2 (April 1937): 147–159.

8. The classic reference is W. A. Phillips, "The Relation Between Unemployment and the Rate of Change of Money Wage Rates in the United Kingdom, 1861–1957," *Economica* 25 (1958): 283–299.

9. My paper on this, "Optimal Employment and Inflation Over Time," first circulated as Cowles Foundation Discussion Paper No. 214 in August 1967, was published later by the London School of Economics under the title "Phillips Curves, Expectation of Inflation and Optimal Unemployment Over Time," *Economica* 34, no. 135 (August 1967): 254–281.

10. Peter Howitt, "Edmund Phelps: Macroeconomist and Social Scientist," *Scandinavia Journal of Economics* 109, no. 2 (March 2007): 203.

11. Axel Leijonhufvud, *The Economics of Keynes and Keynesian Economics* (Oxford: Oxford University Press, 1968).

12. Edmund Phelps, "A Theory of Money Wage Dynamics and Its Implications for the Phillips Curve" (University of Pennsylvania Discussion Paper No. 47, University of Pennsylvania, February 1968); Edmund Phelps, "Money-Wage Dynamics and Labor-Market Equilibrium," *Journal of Political Economy* 76, no. 4, pt. 2: Issues in Monetary Research (July-August 1968): 678–711.

13. Edmund Phelps and Sidney G. Winter, "Optimal Price Policy Under Atomistic Competition," in *Microeconomic Foundations of Employment and Inflation Theory*, ed. Edmund Phelps (New York: Norton, 1970), 309–337.

14. The authors mentioned covered two works that reach the same conclusion: Edmund Phelps, "Phillips Curves"; and Milton Friedman, "The Role of Monetary Policy," *American Economic Review* 58, no. 1 (March 1968): 1–17.

15. Keynes, *General Theory*, 156; Friedrich Hayek, *Individualism and Economic Order*, 3rd ed. (Chicago: University of Chicago Press, 1958), 38–39. The book was originally published in 1948.

16. Philip Cagan, "The Monetary Dynamics of Hyperinflation," in *Studies in the Quantity Theory of Money*, ed. Milton Friedman (Chicago: University of Chicago Press, 1956), 25–117.

17. Edmund Phelps, "Introduction: The New Microeconomics in Employment and Inflation Theory," in *Microeconomic Foundations*, 22.

18. Edmund Phelps and Karl Shell, "Public Debt, Taxation, and Capital Intensiveness," *Journal of Economic Theory* 1, no. 3 (October 1969): 330–346; Edmund Phelps and Edwin Burmeister, "Money, Public Debt, Inflation, and Real Interest," *Journal of Money Credit and Banking* 3, no. 2, pt. 1 (May 1971): 153–182; and Edmund Phelps and Robert Pollak, "On Second-Best National Saving and Game-Equilibrium Growth," *Review of Economic Studies* 35, no. 2 (April 1968): 185–199.

19. Edmund Phelps, "Population Increase," *Canadian Journal of Economics* 1, no. 3 (August 1968): 497–518.

3. UNEMPLOYMENT, WORK'S REWARDS AND JOB DISCRIMINATION

1. Edmund Phelps, *Inflation Policy and Unemployment Theory: The Cost-Benefit Approach to Monetary Planning* (New York: Norton, 1972), xvii.

2. Phelps, *Unemployment Theory*, 113–114.

3. I first used the word in my textbook *Political Economy: An Introductory Text* (New York: Norton, 1985), 44.

4. John Rawls, *A Theory of Justice* (Cambridge, MA: Belknap Press, 1971), 440.

5. Phelps, *Unemployment Theory*, 239.

6. Edmund Phelps, "Phillips Curves, Expectations of Inflation and Optimal Unemployment Over Time," *Economica* 34, no. 135 (August 1967): 254–281.

7. Phelps, *Unemployment Theory*, 238–249.

8. Phelps, *Unemployment Theory*, 244.

9. Phelps, *Unemployment Theory*, 245.

10. Phelps, *Unemployment Theory*, 246.

11. Thomas Nagel arranged for me to give a speech at the annual meeting of the American Philosophical Association, which was subsequently published as "Justice in the Theory of Public Finance," *Journal of Philosophy* 76, no. 11 (November 1979): 677–692.

12. Phelps, *Unemployment Theory*, 25–26.

13. Phelps, *Unemployment Theory*, 659.

14. Phelps, *Unemployment Theory*, 25–26.

15. Edmund Phelps, "The Statistical Theory of Racism and Sexism," *American Economic Review* 62, no. 4 (September 1972): 659.

4. ALTRUISM AND RAWLSIAN JUSTICE

1. Edmund Phelps, "Introduction," in *Altruism, Morality and Economic Theory*, ed. Edmund Phelps (New York: Basic Books, 1975), 2.

2. Phelps, "Introduction," in *Altruism*, 3.

3. Kenneth Arrow, "Gifts and Exchanges," in *Altruism*, 21–22.

4. Peter Hammond, "Charity: Altruism or Cooperative Egoism," in *Altruism*, 130.

5. Phelps, "The Indeterminacy of Game-Equilibrium Growth in the Absence of an Ethic," in *Altruism*, 101.

6. Jerome Foss, "The Hidden Influence of John Rawls," *First Principles*, no. 61, September 22, 2016.

7. Edmund Phelps, "Taxation of Wage Income for Economic Justice," *Quarterly Journal of Economics* 87, no. 3 (August 1973): 331–354.

8. James Mirrlees, "An Exploration in the Theory of Optimum Income Taxation," *Review of Economic Studies* 38, no. 2 (April 1972): 175–208.

9. John Rawls, "The Priority of Right and Ideas of the Good," *Philosophy and Public Affairs* 17, no. 4 (Fall 1988): 257n7.

10. J. A. Ordover, "Distributive Justice and Optimal Taxation of Wages and Interest in a Growing Economy," *Journal of Public Economics* 5, no. 1–2 (January–February 1976): 139–160.

11. Edmund Phelps and J. A. Ordover, "Linear Taxation of Wealth and Wages for Intergenerational Lifetime Justice: Some Steady-State Cases," *American Economic Review* 65 (September 1975): 660–673.

12. Edmund Phelps and John G. Riley, "Rawlsian Growth: Dynamic Programming of Capital and Wealth for Intergenerational 'Maximin' Justice," *Review of Economic Studies* 45, no. 1 (February 1978): 103–120.

13. Philippe Van Parijs, *Real Freedom for All: What (If Anything) Can Justify Capitalism?* (Oxford: Clarendon Press, 1995).

14. Edmund Phelps, "Subsidize Wages: Response to Philippe Van Parijs 'A Basic Income for All,'" *Boston Review*, October 1, 2000.

15. These recent criticism of mine are in my essay "Poverty as Injustice," *Project Syndicate*, August 28, 2020, https://www.project-syndicate.org/commentary/economic-growth-poverty-reduction-role-of-the-state-by-edmund-s-phelps-2020-08.

16. Daron Acemoglu, "Why Universal Basic Income Is a Bad Idea," *Project Syndicate*, June 7, 2019, https://www.project-syndicate.org/commentary/why-universal-basic-income-is-a-bad-idea-by-daron-acemoglu-2019-06?barrier=accesspaylog.

17. Thomas Kuhn, *The Structure of Scientific Revolutions* (Chicago: University of Chicago Press, 1962).

18. Edmund Phelps, *Studies in Macroeconomic Theory*, vol. 1, *Employment and Inflation* (Cambridge, MA: Academic Press, 1979); and Edmund Phelps, *Studies in Macroeconomic Theory*, vol. 2, *Redistribution and Growth* (Cambridge, MA: Academic Press, 1980).

5. SUPPLY-SIDERS, "NEW CLASSICALS" AND AN UN-KEYNESIAN SLUMP

1. Jimmy Carter, "Energy and the National Goals—A Crisis of Confidence," (Speech, Washington, DC, July 15, 1979), American Rhetoric. https://www.americanrhetoric.com/speeches/jimmycartercrisisofconfidence.htm.

2. Robert Mundell, "The Monetary Economics of International Adjustment Under Fixed and Flexible Exchange Rates," *Quarterly Journal of Economics* 74, no. 2 (May 1960): 227–257.

3. Robert Mundell, "Monetary Relations Between Europe and America," in *North American and Western European Economic Policies: Proceedings of the International Economic Association*, ed. C. P. Kindleberger and Andrew Schonfield (London: St. Martin, 1971), 237–256.

4. Mundell's expositions of this thesis were published in "The Dollar and the Policy Mix: 1971" (Essays in International Finance, no. 85, Princeton University Department of Economics, Princeton University, Princeton, NJ, May 1971), 3–34; and "Domestic Financial Policies Under Fixed and Floating Exchange Rates" (staff paper, International Monetary Fund, Washington, DC, November 1962), vol. 9, 369–379.

5. John Brooks, "The Supply Side," *New Yorker*, April 12, 1982.

6. Robert Mundell, "A Reconsideration of the Twentieth Century" (Nobel Prize Lecture, Stockholm, Sweden, December 8, 1999). https://www.nobelprize.org/uploads/2018/06/mundell-lecture.pdf.

7. Paul Samuelson, "The New Look in Tax and Fiscal Policy" in *The Collected Scientific Papers of Paul A. Samuelson*, vol. 2, ed. Joseph Stiglitz (Cambridge, MA: MIT Press, 1966), 1329.

8. In a footnote to his Nobel Prize Lecture, Mundell writes that in the fall of 1968, "the task force of the new Nixon administration recommended, incorrectly in my opinion, tight money [and tight] fiscal policies." I was on that task force, as noted in my memoir of the late 1960s. Although our report advocated a tighter monetary policy, tighter than I had thought we had agreed on, I have no recollection of advocating an austere fiscal policy as well. (The Truman administration had championed fiscal tightness in order to shrink the massive public debt left by World War II and—as Mundell noted—the Kennedy administration proposed legislation of tax cuts.)

9. Edmund Phelps, "Introduction: The New Microeconomics in Employment and Inflation Theory," in *Microeconomic Foundations of Employment and Inflation Theory*, ed. Edmund Phelps (New York: Norton, 1970; London: Macmillan, 1971), 22.

10. Roman Frydman and Edmund Phelps, eds., *Individual Forecasting and Aggregate Outcomes: "Rational Expectations" Examined* (Cambridge: Cambridge University Press, 1983).

11. James Heckman and Sidharth Moktan, "Publishing and Promotion in Economics: The Tyranny of the Top Five," *Journal of Economic Literature* 58, no. 2 (June 2020): 419–470.

12. Edmund Phelps, *Political Economy: An Introductory Text* (New York: Norton, 1985), xiv.

13. Phelps, *Political Economy*, 5.

14. Phelps, *Political Economy*, 108.

15. See Edmund Phelps and Sidney G. Winter, "Optimal Price Policy Under Atomistic Competition," in *Microeconomic Foundations of Employment and Inflation Theory*, 309-337. I did draft and present a last paper at the Bank of Italy, "The Effectiveness of Macropolicies in a Small Open-Economy," Banca d'Italia, Discussion Paper No. 63 (May 1986). This paper was later published in *Money, Macroeconomics, and Economic Policy: Essays in Honor of James Tobin*, ed. William C. Brainard, W. D. Nordhaus, and H. W. Watts (Cambridge, MA: MIT Press, 1991), 125–147.

16. Edmund Phelps and Jean-Paul Fitoussi, "Causes of the Slump in Europe," *Brookings Papers on Economic Activity* 16, no. 2 (December 1986): 497–498.

6. A REVOLUTIONARY DECADE

1. This essay was first published in *Revista di politica economica* 81 (November 1991); subsequently, it was published as Kenneth Arrow and Edmund Phelps, "Proposed Reforms of the Economic System of Information and Decision in the USSR: Commentary and Advice," in *Privatization Processes in Eastern Europe: Theoretical Foundations and Empirical Results*, ed. Mario Baldassarri, Luigi Paganetto, and Edmund Phelps (London: Macmillan, 1993), 15–47.

2. Arrow and Phelps, "Proposed Reforms," 15.

3. Arrow and Phelps, "Proposed Reforms," 20.

4. Arrow and Phelps, "Proposed Reforms," 24.

5. Arrow and Phelps, "Proposed Reforms," 25.

6. See Edmund Phelps, "The Argument for Private Ownership and Control," *Appendix to EBRD Economic Review: World Economic Outlook* (London: European Bank for Reconstruction and Development, September 1993).

7. For the origins of the Mundell-Fleming model, see Robert Mundell, "Capital Mobility and Stabilization Policy Under Fixed and Flexible Exchange Rates," *Canadian Journal of Economics and Political Science* 29, no. 4 (November 1963): 475–485; and J. Marcus Fleming, "Domestic Financial Policies Under Fixed and Floating Exchange Rates," IMF Staff Papers 9 (June 1962): 369–379.

8. My 1968 "Money-Wage Dynamics" paper introducing wage expectations on which to base the "stickiness" of the "money wage" and my 1967 "Phillips Curves" paper introducing price expectations on which to base a sticky inflation rate gave *support* to Keynes's thinking. Edmund

Phelps, "Money-Wage Dynamics and Labor-Market Equilibrium," *Journal of Political Economy* 76, no. 4 (1968): 678–711; "Phillips Curves, Expectations of Inflation, and Optimal Unemployment Over Time," *Economica* 34, no. 135 (1967): 254–281.

9. John Maynard Keynes, "The Balance of Payments of the United States," *Economic Journal* 56, no. 222 (June 1946): 186.

10. A version of that paper is Edmund Phelps, "A Working Model of Slump and Recovery from Disturbances to Capital Goods Demand in an Open Non-Monetary Economy," *America Economic Review* 78, no. 2 (1988): 346–350. Another paper was Edmund Phelps, "Effects of Productivity, Total Domestic-Product Demand, and 'Incentive Wages' on Employment in a Non-Monetary Customer-Market Model of the Small Open Economy," *Scandinavian Journal of Economics* 92, no. 2 (1990): 353–367.

11. A paper Hian Teck and I wrote was published by the *American Economic Review* in 1992; a paper by George and me was published by *Finanz Archiv* in 1994; and Gylfi's Columbia dissertation on some of the statistical testing he did was defended in 1993. Edmund Phelps and Hian Teck Hoon, "Macroeconomic Shocks in a Dynamized Model of the Natural Rate of Unemployment," *American Economic Review* 82, no. 4 (September 1992): 889–900; Edmund Phelps and George Kanaginis, "Fiscal Policy and Economic Activity in the Neoclassical Theory with and without Bequests," *Finanz Archiv* 51, no. 2 (1994): 137–171.

12. Edmund Phelps, with Hian Teck Hoon, George Kanaginis, and Gylfi Zoega, *Structural Slumps: The Modern Equilibrium Theory of Unemployment, Interest, and Assets* (Cambridge, MA: Harvard University Press, 1994), vii–xi.

13. Phelps, *Structural Slumps*, 69.

14. Phelps, *Structural Slumps*, 70.

15. Phelps, *Structural Slumps*, 70–82.

16. Phelps, *Structural Slumps*, 85.

17. For more on the Blanchard-Yaari model, see Olivier J. Blanchard, "Debt, Deficits and Finite Horizons," *Journal of Political Economy* 93 (April 1985): 223–247. For more on the Calvo-Bowles model, see Guillermo A. Calvo, "Quasi-Walrasian Models of Unemployment," *American Economic Review* 69 (May 1979): 102–108; and Samuel Bowles, "A Marxian Theory of Unemployment," (lecture, Columbia University, New York, April 1979).

18. See figure 8.1 in Phelps, *Structural Slumps*, 97.

19. Phelps, *Structural Slumps*, 101.

20. Phelps, *Structural Slumps*, 128–130.

21. Phelps, *Structural Slumps*, 141.

22. Phelps, *Structural Slumps*, 143.

23. Phelps, *Structural Slumps*, 143–144.

24. Phelps, *Structural Slumps*, 144.

25. Phelps, *Structural Slumps*, 311.

26. Phelps, *Structural Slumps*, 311–312.

27. The structure of the model's equations and information on the statistical methods are provided and discussed in section 17.1 of Phelps, *Structural Slumps*, 313–319.

28. Phelps, *Structural Slumps*, 320–321.

29. See Phelps, *Structural Slumps*, 327–329.

30. See Phelps, *Structural Slumps*, 330.

31. See Phelps, *Structural Slumps*, 329.

32. See Phelps, *Structural Slumps*, 342.

33. Phelps, *Structural Slumps*, back cover.

34. Michael Woodford, "Review: Structural Slumps," *Journal of Economic Literature* 32, no. 4 (December 1994): 1784–1815.

35. The *New York Times* piece was by Peter Passell and the *Economist* piece was undoubtedly by Clive Crook.

36. Edmund Phelps, *Rewarding Work: How to Restore Participation and Self-Support to Free Enterprise* (Cambridge, MA: Harvard University Press, 1997), 14.

37. Phelps, *Rewarding Work*, 22.

38. Phelps, *Rewarding Work*, 103–104.

39. Phelps, *Rewarding Work*, 171.

40. Phelps, *Rewarding Work*, 137.

41. Edmund Phelps, "Introduction," in *Designing Inclusion: Tools to Raise Low-End Pay and Employment in Private Enterprise*, ed. Edmund Phelps (Cambridge: Cambridge University Press, 2003), 2–4.

42. Phelps, "Introduction," in *Designing Inclusion*, 2–4.

43. Phelps, "Introduction," in *Designing Inclusion*, 9.

44. Edmund Phelps, "A Strategy for Employment and Growth," *Rivista Italiana degli Economisti* 2, no. 1 (April 1997): 126–128.

45. Phelps, "A Strategy for Employment and Growth," 126–128.

7. A *FESTSCHRIFT*, A NOBEL, AND A NEW HORIZON

1. Paul Samuelson, "Edmund Phelps, Insider-Economists Insider," in *Knowledge, Information, and Expectations in Modern Macroeconomics*, ed. Philippe Aghion, Roman Frydman, Joseph Stiglitz, and Michael Woodford (Princeton, NJ: Princeton University Press, 2003), 1–2.

2. For the full discussion on the "Phelps Program," see Philippe Aghion, Roman Frydman, Joseph Stiglitz, and Michael Woodford, "Edmund Phelps and Modern Macroeconomics," in *Knowledge, Information, and Expectations*, 4–11.

3. Edmund Phelps, "A Life in Economics," in *The Makers of Modern Economics*, vol. 2, ed. A. Heertje (Aldershot, UK: Edward Elgar, 1995), 93. This essay was quoted by the scholar Robert Dimand in his insightful biography, "Edmund Phelps and Modern Macroeconomics," *Review of Political Economy* 20, no. 1 (January 2008.): 23–29.

4. See Thomas Nagel, "Aristotle on Eudaimonia," *Phronesis* 17, no. 3 (1972): 252–259.

5. Edmund Phelps, "Economic Prosperity and the Dynamism of Economic Institutions" (Shaw Foundation Distinguished Lecture, Singapore Management University, Singapore, January 2003; Lecture, Royal Institute of Economic Affairs, London, March 2003), 1–2. This lecture was later published in *The Economic Prospects of Singapore*, eds. W. T. H. Koh and R. Mariano (Singapore: Addison-Wesley, 2005), 299–333.

6. Phelps, "Economic Prosperity and the Dynamism," 10–11.

7. Phelps, "Economic Prosperity and the Dynamism," 10–11.

8. Robert Solow, "A Contribution to the Theory of Economic Growth," *Quarterly Journal of Economics* 70, no. 1 (February 1956): 65–94.

9. Edmund Phelps, "The Economic Performance of Nations" (paper presented at the William Baumol Special Session on Entrepreneurship, Innovation and the Growth Mechanism of the Free-market Economies, 118th Annual Meeting of the American Economic Association, Boston, MA, January 2006), 1–3; later published in *Entrepreneurship, Innovation, and the Growth Mechanism of Free Enterprise Economies*, ed. Eytan Sheshinski, Robert J. Strom, and William J. Baumol (Princeton, NJ: Princeton University Press, 2007): 342–356. (In an email confirming this paper was there with others, among them papers by Arrow and Solow, Eytan remarked it was "a good one, of course.")

10. Phelps, "The Economic Performance of Nations," 3–4.
11. The paper continues,

> Aristotle, in the *Nicomachean Ethics*, starts from the premise that "all men desire knowledge" and goes on to discuss the relations among work, learning, development, enjoyment and happiness. Cellini in his *Autobiography* is the prototype of the liberated individualist bent on accomplishment and success. Smith propounds the social value of self-help and competition, and he champions broad participation in such a business life. Say extols entrepreneurs as constantly reinventing the economy in their quest for higher yields and Condorcet elevates the productivity of these economic entrepreneurs over the zero-sum results of political entrepreneurs vying for political favor. Evidently American values derive from this European thought. And this line of thought goes on beyond the 18th century. In later centuries, Henri Bergson sees the potential for change as the *elan vital* and [sees] the good life as one of constant "becoming" rather than mere "being." Marshall dwells on the workplace as the source of most of people's mental activity and Myrdal views jobs as soon to be a richer source of most people's satisfaction than their consumption.

> See Phelps, "The Economic Performance of Nations," 4.

12. Edmund Phelps, "Toward a Model of Innovation and Performance Along the Lines of Knight, Keynes, Hayek and M. Polanyi" (paper presented at the Max Planck Institute's Conference on Entrepreneurship and Economic Growth, Rinbgerg Castle in Tegernsee, Germany, May 8–9, 2006), 1–5; later published in *Entrepreneurship, Growth, and Public Policy*, ed. Zoltan J. Acs, David B. Audretsch, and Robert Strom (Cambridge: Cambridge Press, 2009): 35–70.
13. Phelps, "Toward a Model of Innovation," 5–6.
14. Phelps, "Toward a Model of Innovation," 5–6.
15. Phelps, "Toward a Model of Innovation," 12.
16. Phelps, "Toward a Model of Innovation," 14–15.
17. Phelps, "Toward a Model of Innovation," 14–15.
18. Phelps, "Toward a Model of Innovation," 15–16.
19. Phelps, "Toward a Model of Innovation," 23.

20. Phelps, "Toward a Model of Innovation," 24.
21. Phelps, "Toward a Model of Innovation," 24.
22. This caught the attention of *Project Syndicate* in my "Say More" interview on May 4, 2021.

8. THE GREAT WAVE OF INDIGENOUS INNOVATION, MEANINGFUL WORK, AND THE GOOD LIFE

1. Friedrich Hayek, "The Use of Knowledge in Society" *American Economic Review* 35, no. 4 (September 1945): 523–524.
2. Edmund Phelps, *Mass Flourishing: How Grassroots Innovation Created Jobs, Challenge, and Change* (Princeton, NJ: Princeton University Press, 2013), 31–32.
3. Michael Polanyi, *Personal Knowledge: Toward a Post-Critical Philosophy* (London: Routledge and Kegan Paul, 1958, 1962), 5.
4. Edmund Phelps, "Population Increase," *Canadian Journal of Economics* 1, no. 3 (1968): 497–518.
5. Phelps, *Mass Flourishing*, ini.
6. Phelps, *Mass Flourishing*, ix, 19–20.
7. Phelps, *Mass Flourishing*, 27–28.
8. Abraham Lincoln, "Second Lecture on Discoveries and Inventions," February 11, 1859, Young Men's Association of Bloomington, IL.
9. See Frank Taussig, "Some Aspects of the Tariff Question," *Quarterly Journal of Economics* 3, no. 1 (April 1889): 259–292. See also his 1915 of the same title.
10. To borrow from a lecture title of Leonard Bernstein.
11. Phelps, *Mass Flourishing*, 97–98.
12. Phelps, *Mass Flourishing*, 29.
13. Phelps, *Mass Flourishing*, 98–99.
14. Phelps, *Mass Flourishing*, 99–100.
15. Phelps, *Mass Flourishing*, 100.
16. Phelps, *Mass Flourishing*, 101.
17. Phelps, *Mass Flourishing*, 101.
18. Phelps, *Mass Flourishing*, 280–282.
19. Phelps, *Mass Flourishing*, 269.
20. Phelps, *Mass Flourishing*, 211–212.
21. See Phelps, *Mass Flourishing*, 9ni1.

22. For a more robust exposition see Phelps, *Mass Flourishing*, 26–27.

23. For the Spiethoff-Solow model see Arthur Spiethoff, "Krisen," in *Handworterbuch der Sozialwissenschaften*, vol. 6, ed. L. Elster, A. Weber, and F. Wieser (Jena: G. Fischer, 1923), 8–91; and Robert Solow, "A Contribution to the Theory of Economic Growth," *Quarterly Journal of Economics* 70, no. 1 (February 1956): 65–94. For the Aghion-Howitt model see Philippe Aghion and Peter W. Howitt, *Endogenous Growth Theory* (Cambridge, MA: MIT Press 1997). See also *The Economics of Creative Destruction*, ed. Ufuk Akcigit and John Van Reenen (Cambridge, MA: Harvard University Press, 2022); as well as Richard R. Nelson and Sidney G. Winter, *An Evolutionary Theory of Economic Change* (Cambridge, MA: Harvard University Press, 1982).

24. Edmund Phelps, "Economic Culture and Economic Performance: What Light Is Shed on the Continent's Problem" (working paper 17, Conference of CESifo and Center on Capitalism and Society, Columbia University, Venice, Italy, July 21–22, 2006), 12.

25. Phelps, "Economic Culture and Economic Performance," 11.

26. The construction of this index is explained in *Mass Flourishing*, 212; the relationship is shown in the scatter-point diagram, figure 8.5, *Mass Flourishing*, 214.

27. In order of appearance: I wrote the Introduction, Raicho wrote Part One (chapters 1–3, also 6), Gylfi wrote Part Two (chapters 4–5 and 7), and Hian Teck wrote Part Three (chapters 8–10).

28. Edmund Phelps, Raicho Bojilov, Hian Teck Hoon, and Gylfi Zoega, *Dynamism: The Values That Drive Innovation, Job Satisfaction, and Economic Growth* (Cambridge, MA: Harvard University Press, 2020), 22.

29. Phelps, Bojilov, Hoon, and Zoega, *Dynamism*, 24.

30. Phelps, Bojilov, Hoon, and Zoega, *Dynamism*, 26.

31. Phelps, Bojilov, Hoon, and Zoega, *Dynamism*, 28.

32. For the relationship between innovation and high job satisfaction, see table 7.1 in Phelps, Bojilov, Hoon, and Zoega, *Dynamism*, 146; for the relationship between innovation and happiness, see figure 7.3, *Dynamism*, 148.

33. See table 1.1 in Phelps, Bojilov, Hoon, and Zoega, *Dynamism*, 42.

34. Phelps, *Mass Flourishing*, 324.

35. Richard Robb, *Willful: How We Choose What We Do* (New Haven, CT: Yale University Press, 2019), 191.

EPILOGUE

1. A phrase of Molly Worthen's in her article "A Thinker's Life," *Yale Alumni Magazine*, July/August 2021.

2. Richard Robb, *Willful: How We Choose What We Do* (New Haven, CT: Yale University Press, 2019), 17.

3. Amartya Sen, *Home in the World: A Memoir* (London: Allen Lane, 2021).

4. Remarks and direct quotes from the preface to Edmund Phelps, *Structural Slumps: The Modern Equilibrium Theory of Unemployment, Interest, and Assets* (Cambridge, MA: Harvard University Press, 1994), xii.

INDEX